How to Win the Conference

How to Win the Conference

by WILLIAM D. ELLIS
and FRANK SIEDEL

illustrated by Robert Mowry

PRENTICE HALL, INC.
ENGLEWOOD CLIFFS, N.J. 07632

PRINTED IN THE UNITED STATES OF AMERICA

0-13-439489-5

*To Martha and Thomas
and their families,
and to our teachers—
men in industry who get
the world's work done by
enabling people to see
eye to eye on projects
of importance.*

Table of Contents

Foreword ix

1. "Let's Start the Argument" 1
2. The Argument 10
3. How a Conference Becomes a Hassle . . 19
4. The First Rule 24
5. Recognition Test 29
6. Uncommon Sense in the Internal Meeting . 35
7. Imagination in the Conference . . . 43
8. Some Masters of the Conference . . . 51
9. Let's Start 65
10. Things to Look for When You Hire a
    Management 75
11. The Empty Chair 83
12. Humor in the Conference 94
13. It's All in How You Say It 100
14. How to Take Over a Job 109
15. "How to Lose One" 113
16. Hire the President 117
17. Timing 129

18. Don't Be a Stranger 136
19. Some Autocrats of the Conference Table . 146
20. Is This Conference Necessary? . . . 158
21. Be Prepared 163
22. Telephone Conference 169
23. Who Are You Working For? 179
24. The Irate Delegation 187
25. Man the Lookouts 198
26. How to Close a Conference 208
27. A Word in Private 211

Foreword

THIS IS NOT a polite book. There are well-mannered books on the subject of conferring which begin with such statements as: "A conference is held for the purpose of *exchanging ideas.*"

This book disagrees. Let us not be naive. A work-a-day business conference is no such thing. It is for the purpose of cramming *one* idea through someone else's objections. To "exchange ideas" is no part of the object of anyone important in the conference we are discussing.

We are not here to study the annual conference on the Advancement of Cactus Garden Culture. There perhaps they go to "exchange ideas." But to exchange ideas is very easy and very unimportant because people who have time to go to a meeting for the express purpose of "exchanging ideas" have no urgent ideas to exchange. Those who have ideas of urgency are out trying to railroad them through someone else's stubbornness . . . usually for money.

The writers are not laughing arrogantly at this "exchange of ideas" concept. It is a logical misunderstanding because it is implicit in the true definition of the word "conference." The word should be changed to "argument," dispassionately, as a lawyer uses the word.

But meanwhile thousands of business men are lulled to sleep by the very word "conference" which is a complete misnomer. And while they sleep, those who know better are making hay at the expense of the sleeper.

The purpose of this book is to wake this sleeper to the practical definition of "conference." We said jokingly that the very name should be changed from "conference" to "argument." But we were not really joking. So . . . let's start the argument.

The Authors

How to Win the Conference

1

"Let's Start the Argument"

A MAN IN OHIO has a plan for local water conservation control which will alleviate water shortage, industrial and municipal. The hydraulic engineering is worked out in detail and reviewing technicians agree that it is workable. The finances are worked out to amortize conventionally. Everything seems to be in order.

But a roomful of twelve legislators must be persuaded that the plan warrants authorization. After the six years of labor which has gone in the planning, this part should be easy. But it is not. The plan is rejected. The complex engineering was successfully handled. The simple conference was not.

An advertising copywriter comes up with a striking campaign for one of the clients of his agency. It is such a natural that his enthusiasm drives him to lay out the campaign on paper, with pictures and copy. He knows that the six men who must approve the campaign will see the merit of it instantly, even though it involves

1

a slight change in their customary advertising. It will merely be a matter of calling them together for a half hour conference.

But the six men do not see it. The idea later returns astonishing results to a competitor who came upon the same idea. But our man never got it through the conference.

A designer has an idea for a reclining front seat for automobiles. Testing his idea on other people, he finds literally hundreds who have had the same experience as he. "If only there were some way the man sitting beside the driver could lean back and sleep while the other drives . . ."

People recount their attempts to lean their heads against the top of the front seat. But it is too low. They try leaning against the side. But the partition between the windows is too hard and vibrates against their heads.

The designer makes detailed specifications of his reclining auto seat. He asks for a hearing on the idea at Pontiac. They give him all the time he wants and a good hearing.

But they don't see it. Nash comes out with it six months later. He succeeded with the product, failed with the conference.

And farther down the corporate ladder, a bright accountant develops a system of estimating the amount of ore in a given stockpile, using a carefully scaled aerial photograph. The system is geometrical and will save the company thousands of dollars a year. He tries the method on several kinds of stockpiled ores. Each time his figures check out with conventional and more laborious methods. He asks his fellow accountants to find holes in it. There are none. The method is such an obvious improvement that it requires only a meeting with the president, comptroller and executive vice president. They will adopt it instantly.

But they do not.

It turns out that *the conference* makes all the difference. This is nothing new. It's an old story.

A man named John Fitch spent a lifetime developing a boat which would propel itself over water. It was powered by a steam engine. It was obvious to John Fitch and to many others that such a boat would open up the American West by making full upstream use of all arteries of the great Mississippi water system. It was only a matter of showing his model to a Mr. Don Diego and a certain General George Washington. Any man could see that eight miles an hour upstream would build an American empire of trade.

But they did not see it.

A certain painter of miniature pictures came along, however, to witness Fitch's experiments. He could not match John Fitch as an engineer, but he was far better skilled than the conscientious, cantankerous Fitch at pushing an idea through a conference.

Using the same facts as Fitch had used, with less documentation and familiarity, the picture painter persuaded financiers to invest in a steamboat.

Result: John Fitch died penniless; the picture painter has enjoyed a century and a half of fame as the inventor of the steamboat . . . Robert Fulton.

The list is long.

A year or a lifetime of solid, skillful, earnest endeavor is easily wiped out in a half hour conference which is not well handled.

We do not study the art of conferring. We study engineering, law, accounting, salesmanship, business administration. We study materials, methods, traffic management, marketing, materials handling, taxation. But we do not study the business of "conferring," where all these other apparently more productive skills must come to trial.

The writers do not admire the need to study the business of conferring. But it is a fact to be faced. It is much more admirable to become a superior engineer, a superior salesman, accountant, lawyer. But increasingly these abilities are wasted without the ability to handle the conference in which one's skills are accepted or rejected today.

A man's ability to get his job of engineering done . . . to get his job of accounting done . . . may well depend upon his ability to navigate skillfully through the intricate maze of conferences which moves the great corporate body today. This ability often outweighs in importance his ability to engineer, sell, produce, finance, execute or transport; because if he has not the ability to handle the all-powerful, omnipresent American conference, he will not get the chance to engineer, sell, finance or produce.

To the earnest, busy engineer or accountant or ship's captain this state of affairs is a crime and a nuisance. He recognizes the truth of it, but he is so impatient with conferences that even here on page 5 he is loath to admit it. Such a man is admirable. But his impatience and his loathing will not make it go away. The conference is here to stay and to increase in importance.

A good man despises to admit that mere talking could become paramount to his first love . . . his constructive, contributive skill—his profession. Therefore the reasons for this state of affairs must be spelled out and they must be overwhelming. They are.

The reasons:

1) When you have spent ten years and perhaps $10,000 or $10,000,000 trying to make each employee see his importance, you have created a man to whom you do not successfully issue orders. With this man you reason. This means conference.

2) We are increasingly specialists. In the beginning the owner and founder of a company was the president. He was also the head of production. He was the salesman, and he handled the financing. He had to confer with no one to borrow money, call on a customer or change the product.

But today we have specialized to the point where the owner is not the president, he is only the owner. And usually he is only the owner of a small part of the corporation . . . a stockholder. The president is someone else, and he is so specialized that he has not even met the owner, only the owner's representative on the board of directors.

Within this corporation are salesmen, who only sell, engineers who only engineer, production men who neither sell nor develop, but only produce what others have sold or developed. And among these production men we find a specialized production man who produces only electric motors. And working for him are men who produce only the armatures of the motors. And for this latter man works another who produces only armatures for AC motors, not DC motors. And for this man works a man who produces only the shaft for this armature, and still another who only inspects to see that this next-to-last man did it right.

And between the owner who only owns and this last man who only inspects, there lie a thousand conferences. For the conference is the only mechanism by which the president of the company can see that the specialized motor which was sold to the customer by the specialist salesman does actually get produced by the specialist production man, and does contain an armature which is bound to a shaft made by the specialist shaft maker, so that the specialist owner gets his dividend mailed to him by the specialist accountant.

To see that the shaft fits the armature, the armature fits the motor, the motor fits the salesman's customer . . . there are conferences. And they will increase because . . .

3) Our corporations, our armies, our governments are constantly increasing in size . . . along with our population. Yet the time-tested rule of thumb that one man can only directly lead twelve other men, still stands. Thus it may be seen that a corporation president can

successfully lead twelve division heads; and these twelve among them can handle together 144 executives; and these 144 can successfully lead 1,728 other executives, and we are not yet even down to the production floor.

But when our corporation expands, say to twenty-four divisions, then our president installs between himself and the division heads two other multi-division vice presidents who each control twelve divisions or twelve staff functions. And this multiplicity of personnel increases all down the line necessitating further conferences and liaison so that the generators made in division A will feed the motors made in division B through electric cable made in division C via the transformers made in division D . . . and so on up to division twenty-four.

And while the conferences increase among the heads of divisions A, B, and C, they also increase on sub-assembly line F in division A where the man who makes the shaft for the AC armature has broken his job down to two men, one who still makes the shaft for the AC armature; the other makes almost the same shaft but modified to fit the new product made in division twenty-four.

Thus conferences.

4) *Outside services.* This increase in corporate size fosters the use of outside specialists. If our company is making electrical apparatus, it wants to confine itself to the electrical apparatus business. It does not want to go into the accounting business, the law business, the police business.

It therefore hires specialist firms to handle its account-

ing, litigation, personnel work, financing, plant main-
tenance and police.

To deal with all these suppliers requires constant
conferences in which the suppliers are advised or in-
spired, are approved or rejected.

The reader by now perhaps has been enough reminded
of his own experiences to be nodding his head with a
sigh, conceding even to himself that the business of his
company involves conferences at every turn. If he is completely honest he is remembering that in many instances
the ability to handle these multitudinous conferences has
made the difference in his company between the administrative executives and the policy executives.

His mind has perhaps wandered beyond his own company to the national leaders. He perhaps has reflected
that General Eisenhower never had the combat command
experience of a Montgomery or a Patton. As a specialist
in the trade of war he was outranked by Generals Arnold,
Krueger and Bradley. General Eisenhower was known,
though, as a man who could get people together; he
could sell a joint effort through a meeting; he could
unify divergent attitudes. He could confer. When they
went looking for the man to head the allied forces they
didn't pick the top artilleryman, the top infantryman,
the top airman, the top admiral. They picked the top
conferrer.

The president of U.S. Steel, left to his own resources,
could probably not make a pound of steel. But when
labor wants a raise and stockholders want dividends
and the government wants the rest, there are always

meetings, conferences. He has had success in such meetings. His presidency of the world's largest steel company has been attributed to this ability.

Your company . . . is it headed by the man who can best handle your product? Or by the man who can best handle your people?

Now the handling of people in the broad sense is not presumed to be treated here. But the formal arena or stage where this effort comes to climax is the conference, to which important subject we give no formal study. We should.

That is the purpose of this book.

2

The Argument

HALF THE SKILL of a good man at a conference lies in realizing that it *is* a contest. Some will come out the winners, some the losers.

Admittedly this phrasing is severe. It suggests a sharp and hostile division of opinion and interests. In many conferences the winnings and the losses are so soft and subtle and small that they are hardly evident, and many leave the room without the faintest feeling that anyone has won or lost anything. Perfect civility, even geniality, has governed. It has been a pleasant and sociable interlude in the morning.

This is as it should be. And a man should not enter a conference with the order of battle written out on paper, nor on his face, nor too much on his mind.

But most people err in the opposite direction. Because of the friendly manner in which they have been asked to be present, because of a lifetime conditioning to a courteous society, and because the words have all been pleasant, many men enter and leave a hundred conferences without any real understanding of the basic conflicts in any of them.

Such men are genial lambs strolling through a slaughter house. Because we wear business suits, because we are called "Mister," and because no man lays a hand on us from morning until night, we are lulled away from the elemental understanding of competing which we had only a few years back.

As schoolboys we understood these things better. We wore suits and ties then, too, and we ate with our left arms off the table when our team went as guests to the opponents' training table for lunch before the game.

When we dressed in the gym one of the opponents took each of our men to a locker. As we went out onto the field our host would clap us on the back and say, "Good luck."

The highest good nature prevailed over the toss of the coin and the choosing of goals. But when the first sweat was up, the man who so recently clapped you on the back now drove his shoulder into your stomach. And that made everything clear-cut. It was a contest, understood, and you were free to fight.

And within your own squad, two fraternity brothers hammered helmets for the left guard berth. They understood about the contest.

Later in combat in World Wars I and II and II ½, three generations of us learned the release of total energy into the winning of a point, where the loser lost everything.

But in business the contest becomes clouded under the common graces to the point that many a man goes through half a business career with his guard down, self-righteously proclaiming that all conferences are "just a lot of talk and wasted time." For him, they have been.

But if a conference was called, there was a point at contest. This meeting was called for a reason. Something was bought or sold—an idea, a plan or a product. Something was up for selection or rejection. There was opposition present—tacit or otherwise. If this were not so, no meeting would have been called.

At about this point you are thinking, "This is not always so. I have been to plenty of meetings where there was no issue. There was no decent reason for calling the meeting. Or the conference was called just to pass out some information, or to 'exchange ideas.'"

You may remember these incidents:

1) "Fred Murphy called a conference of all the engineering development men. He's taking over as laboratory director. No one ever was able to tell what the meeting was all about. It was just a meeting."

2) "Mr. Trent called a meeting. But there's never any contest when old man Trent speaks. He just lays down the law."

3) "Sam Berker held a meeting. But that was just to tell us the new way he's going to handle executive salaries. No contest. Just dissemination of company policy."

No contest? Yes, sir. These are not the kinds of conferences this book is designed to help most. But they

are chosen here because they seem to challenge the premise that a conference is a contest. They are sleepers. But make no mistake, these were contests.

Take number one, Fred Murphy. No one was able to tell why the meeting was called. But there are many possible reasons. The most likely is that Fred Murphy called that meeting to establish himself. Murphy may have had no message for the laboratory engineers, other than the implicit message, "Notice who it is now that calls meetings in this division."

It may have been a still fainter motive. Perhaps informality and vagueness of assignment in the laboratory had gone so far that Murphy felt a meeting would firm up the lab. Perhaps individuals working on separate projects had developed so much autonomy that he felt the lab was becoming too decentralized and independent. The meeting would point up the organization lines and smarten up the consciousness of the unity of the laboratory.

Perhaps Fred Murphy already knows that two months from now he will want to call a meeting on an explosive subject. He wants to establish a routine of meetings so that his "big" meeting won't cause a stir.

If Fred Murphy even felt the necessity of calling the meeting, there was a contest. A faint contest perhaps for authority, perhaps a contest between Fred Murphy and himself. He may even have needed to show someone *outside* the lab that he controlled the group. But make no mistake, it was a contest. And when it was over somebody had won or lost a point.

Let's look at number two. Mr. Trent merely called

in the men and dictated the new sales quotas. Trent has perhaps through the years beaten the appearance of contest out of it. But if a man calls in his executives to lay down the law, and if they accept it, he has won a contest. For a half dozen men cannot always, on all things, agree with one other man. But if they always *accept* his dictates, Mr. Trent wins a contest each time. And his victory is cumulative.

Number three. Sam Berker explains the new salary policy. Merely informative? No. If Sam Berker succeeds in explaining his new policy, if he makes it clear, he has won a contest—even if it is only a contest for your understanding. It is more likely, though, that he needs not only your understanding, but your *acceptance*. What he lays out in arbitrary terms as an accomplished policy may in fact need your active cooperation or support to become effective. Sam Berker is more likely covering a selling job in the guise of a statement of fact. The board may have said, "It's all right with us, Sam, if you can make it work."

He is outlining "Company Policy." But for the moment assume that there is no such thing as "the company." There are only individual men, Sam Berker being one of them. So what comes under the armor-clad label of "Company Policy" is only the plan or idea of Sam Berker. It will not become "Company Policy" unless you let it. And if Sam makes policies which the other executives will contest or quietly resist, then it becomes apparent to all that Sam Berker is no policy maker. And Sam knows this.

For the most part, though, the contest in a conference

is not so faint as these. It is not necessary or suggested that you enter the conference with a predetermined bias or opinion. Go in, if you wish, for "the exchange of ideas." Just be aware that whatever it looks like, it *is* a contest. With that understanding your business career will take on new sharpness, direction, and vitality. You will enter a thrilling game.

Perhaps the discussion does not affect you or your department directly, but you will get more out of the meeting if you realize that it *is*—any conference *is*—a contest.

The point won may be so small that you don't mind if Murphy does win it. But the cumulative weight of winning a number of such contests creates a leader who is able to win larger and sharper contests. Will you grant this to Murphy as willingly? Or do you want it for yourself?

The semiconscious executive slumbers blandly through these seemingly innocuous meetings which can be more vital than the budget meetings, policy meetings, purchase meetings where the conflict is obvious to all.

Be Able to Recognize a Conference

After understanding that any conference is a contest, be able to recognize a conference when you see one.

When the manager's secretary calls and asks, "Would you hold open one hour at 2:30 on Wednesday to discuss budgets with Mr. Adam" . . . that's obviously a conference. But often they're not labeled so clearly.

"Bill! You going down for cigarettes? Wait, I'll come along. Want to ask you about the delivery dates on the turbines anyhow." That's a conference, too.

That's all right. Talk while you go down for cigarettes. It's a good relaxed atmosphere for discussion. Saves time, too. Just be aware he's going to ask for faster delivery for his special customer on those turbines. We don't care whether you agree to it or refuse. Our only interest is that you recognize the contest, the conference.

"Bill, you busy? You might want to sit in upstairs. Man from Targ & Company giving us a mighty interesting presentation on southern markets."

Maybe you're not busy. Maybe you'd like to hear the presentation. That's all right. Just understand you're going into a contest.

It may not involve you. But the man from Targ & Company is not here for pure sociability. Chances are he's selling some kind of service to your company. That's a contest.

Chances are good that some of your people like what he's selling. Some don't. Chances are, too, the man who so casually invited you along has quite pointed ideas on southern markets. Chances are he asked you along because someone else has equally pointed and opposite ideas. He wants you along to bolster his side.

"Bill, come down to the shipping department with me. Need your advice about something."

Maybe he needs your advice. Maybe he doesn't. Either

way it's a contest. He may want two against one against the man in charge of shipments, and he already knows how you stand. Or he may want to point out an improvement which you can furnish, which will help him.

Perhaps he really does wish plain advice from plain motives. If so, fine. The only thing necessary at this point is: if it's a conference, recognize it. Because it's also a contest.

A conference may be just a chance meeting at the elevator button. It may be the interruption that calls you out of a big meeting for a brief exchange in the hall. Recognize it, and don't sleep through it.

3

How a Conference Becomes
a Hassle

THIS IS A COMPENDIUM of stock words, clichés and attitudes which can turn any armed truce into declared war.

Policy level readers will think such specifics beneath them until they remember how many times within their experience "policy" has come down to a question of the shade of red in somebody's temples, caused by somebody waving the flag words:

> "*Now let's get back to basics.*" This remark will get you *back* all right . . . *way* back. Admittedly you must get the meeting back on the track. But this particular phraseology has been used so often, and so smugly, by men who have thought they were the only ones in the room to perceive the digression, that the user of these words inherits all the unpleasant associations

19

his conferees have had in meetings over the years. The writer has heard many good ways of getting a meeting back to the point, and it is easy to devise others. But they should be individualized and native to the speaker's own personality and character.

Take a pencil and, in the margin of this page, invent two better ways of saying this. You will use them before a week has passed. Make one serious, the other jovial, good-natured kidding.

"I can't buy that!" The vogue for this expression will pass a few months after this book is published. But there will be another to replace it. Any of these stock expressions which come into heavy parlance handicap the user. By this particular one, you set yourself up as being in a position "to buy" or "not to buy." And it is usually used by a man who has not the authority to exert a simple "No." Whether you can or not, no credit accrues to you for playing the heavy "buyer" role.

Any of these fad expressions brands you with the provincialism of the moment. You also inherit all the unpleasant associations the listeners have with the phrase.

Use your own natural expressions and retain your individuality.

"Now let's look at this thing from all angles."
If this is a preface to some specific objection

or proposal . . . go ahead, if you must. But it exasperates every man in the room because it is usually uttered by a speaker who has no firm opinion one way or the other, but who has a native fear of decisions quickly reached. It is also often the cry of the man who has waded out over his head.

If the point is worth arguing, it has probably been looked at from all angles. If it hasn't, it probably isn't worth so many looks. The all-angle looker usually means, "Wait till I catch up."

But if you think the proposition has not been thoroughly considered, better to call on a specific individual . . . "Fred, how's this going to work out from the taxation viewpoint?"

"Hassle." Don't say the word. Maybe it is a hassle, but as soon as someone says the word that makes it official. A kind of resignation sets in around the table, and disappointment.

From that moment work becomes difficult to accomplish. Pessimism about the meeting defeats the meeting.

The same applies to all the substitute words, of course, such as: *palaver, yak-yak, talking-in-circles, splitting hairs.*

"Now look, Jones." Even good old Jonesey's neck hair will usually stiffen up if you use his bare last name. He had to put up with that in the army or the navy, but from you, he doesn't.

If you know him well, that's one thing. But if you don't, call him familiarly or call him Mister.

"Now I don't know where we got our signals crossed, but . . ." This assures everyone that you know very well it isn't your side who's wrong, and it takes you a couple notches closer to zero. If you're trying to fix it, say, "Now, look, I know very well we can get this thing back on the good track we started with." Follow it up with what your side is willing to do and then ask the other side very directly to do something specific.

You'll be hard to deny.

"On this condition." Not the best way to start off a delicate proposition.

"What does your Mr. Johnson think of this?" To ask a man what his boss thinks of an idea is a good way to raise the thermometer ten degrees in any conference room.

4

The First Rule

UNDERSTAND THIS: that if you take face from *any* man in the room . . . you lose.

Many a policy has been safely strongarmed through a conference, only to find that it won't work in the field. The *unimportant* gentleman from "downstairs" sees to that. His self-respect was left in shreds the day of the policy meeting. He has turned around and shredded the policy. He may not even know he did this.

Or, if the weight of influence is all on your side, maybe there's nothing he can do to hurt this time. But you still lose. He's already lined up with the opposition for the next time you come through, when you have a weaker case. And there *will* be a next time. There always is. The world is that small.

"That makes it next to impossible!" you say. "How can you ram your idea through another man's opposition without his losing face? You'd have to be superhuman!"

Granted. And now you're just beginning to see the importance of the conference skill and this book.

The First Skill

Since it is necessary to guard the other man's pride, though opposing him, it is necessary to recognize that every person in that room has an objective. Count the number of men in that room and you have counted the number of axes which must be ground today.

The unsuccessful conferee often assumes that there are two or three important men or points of view in the room, and the others are just along to fill up the chairs.

The successful conferee is the man who recognizes each man's stake and gives each something to take home with him.

This is not so hard to do as it seems. But it takes alertness. Most of these axes are not big axes. And the man who is sensitive to their presence can often sharpen the smaller ones effortlessly, in passing, with one hand tied behind his back. He can often sharpen enough of the small ones to cut the handle off the big one.

Most of the axes to be sharpened are only matters of pride.

Let's set up a sample meeting. There are eight men in the room. Everyone knows the principals are Anderson and *you*. Anderson wants the advertising budget spent at headquarters, nationally. You want it spent regionally or by districts.

Anderson directs all his remarks and his arguments at you. He ignores the less formidable contenders in the room. But you look over the field to see what axes are to be ground. Never mind what you'll do about them at present. Just let's see what you can sense or deduce about the others in the room.

There's that brand-new young assistant of Anderson's whom Anderson didn't even bother to introduce to you. What does he want out of this meeting? Not very much. But at least he probably wants a chance to register well today in Anderson's eyes. You can help him do this even as he opposes you. Listen while he talks. Commend his best arguments even as you parry them. Congratulate Anderson jovially on having such a man on his side.

On the other side of Anderson is Miller, long-time assistant to Anderson but much overshadowed. Through years of being in Anderson's shade, he might seem resigned to such a role. Don't you believe it.

He's long since resigned perhaps to not having much say about this matter, but there is no man who does not crave respect. If he's entitled to it give him a handful of that precious stuff.

At the end of the table is Bradford. He seems to favor Anderson's idea of central handling of advertising, with or without much conviction. But you remember also that Bradford has recently come into headquarters from the districts. He has on occasion taken stands which gave him something of a reputation as the man with "the district viewpoint." He has been somewhat cast in this role; apparently it's his strength. Trade on that.

Sample: "Brad, you're the watchdog for the districts around here. I remember you telling me that a man in

New York can't possibly get the feel of the Kansas City market. So let's have our Kansas City advertising handled by a Kansas City man."

Sample: "If we handled the advertising regionally we could still exercise enough control to suit everyone. Brad could go out to the districts from time to time. He has good acceptance with them, so he could guide them. Be a chance to keep Brad well known in each district headquarters."

On your left is Martinson. What does he want? He's afraid that the fine campaign he laid out will be tossed aside if advertising is handled regionally. He sees his function lessened.

Let's face it: to gain Martinson's support you must make a plan in which he can function with satisfaction. Perhaps you can show him how his usefulness will be *increased* by such a move. Otherwise you must win your point without him. Perhaps you can. But decide.

Let's look over at McGuire. He's the one chewing the inside of his cheek nervously and thoughtfully. He represents your advertising agency. By the decentralization of the advertising he sees himself losing the account. McGuire has one of the larger axes to be ground at this table. And his sense of preservation tells him to use it to chop the chair right out from under you. But on the other hand, if you can somehow sharpen McGuire's axe you'll have a powerful ally.

This seems difficult, but don't rule out the possibility. Perhaps you can upgrade McGuire's thinking, show him how he needn't lose the account at all. Perhaps this

provides him with a natural springboard to put his agency
on the national basis. Show him how he could open one-
man offices in each of your districts. Perhaps he has had
to turn down other accounts because he has not had
branch offices. Lift him up.

Perhaps it is not necessary for him to open branch
offices. From his central location perhaps he can handle
the purchasing of advertising space and also direct the
creative advertising.

Perhaps he can assign one man to travel the districts
and earn an increase in the budget. Before you enter
the room, study the hopes and fears of McGuire. See if
you can figure out how your proposal can make him
better off.

If this is not possible, then of course prepare to meet
him head on.

There will be others in the room. Project yourself inside
each of them. Look at your own proposal through their
eyes. *Empathy* . . . is the word for that. *And it is the one
word which summarizes the whole art of the conference.*

5

Recognition Test

IT IS PRESUMPTUOUS to lump human beings into types, of course; but it is only a little bit presumptuous. That people fall into type is at least true enough that Al Capp could make his fortune by caricaturing, in only a dozen characters, most of the kinds of people in Dogpatch or in North America. They are so instantly recognizable that several million readers supported Mr. Capp in good style.

It goes against our training and our better judgment to make hasty estimates of people. But we do it all the time. We just don't admit it, we don't write it down in black and white. We do it because it is necessary to do it.

To size up one's opponent quickly is the essence of any contest. Often success depends upon the accuracy of this split-second estimate. A rifleman capturing an armed prisoner of war estimates the intentions of his enemy and either pulls the trigger or holds his fire. In a hundredth of a second the professional boxer estimates the courage of his opponent . . . with a bluff punch. A broken field runner may make ten such decisions in the course of fifty seconds or in fifty yards; and an attorney before the bar exercising his pre-emptory jury challenge often decides after one sweeping glance at twelve men. That's all the time he has. So let's not be squeamish about typing people in a conference.

Conferences have their own special types. Or the conference brings out similar qualities in different men. It is useful to recognize this for, by the signs, one can often decide accurately what to expect from each in the way of help or damage.

> *The Bull*: Bless him. Whether he's for you or against you, you usually know exactly where he stands . . . in loud unequivocal terms.

He may be bright or dull-witted, but he is always courageous. He is worth much of your time, whether he's at the head of the table or the foot; and he is likely to be at one extreme or the other.

> *The Beaver:* The Beaver is recognized by several signs. And he is not worthy of your main effort. He will be very busy, very attentive, and his bright-eyed attention may invite you to concentrate your communication toward him. But he may be a very light weight indeed.

He is likely to be the one who arranged for the conference room. He is likely to be the one who immediately places a pad and pencil in front of himself. Even before

anything has happened, he begins to write. He has likely written: "Meeting on district sales . . . July 9th. Present: Messrs. Brown, Jamison, Watson, Kovac, Bronson."

This scurrying is often for somebody's benefit, or it is substitution for real worth, or it is often to excuse himself from participation in the later "hot-and-heavy" parts of the meeting. He is the self-appointed secretary of the meeting.

This pad also gives him a place to rest his eyes when a commitment is required of him later. When a searching gaze around the table requests agreement, an opinion, or a nod, the Beaver will be busy making notes. Nobody knows what he writes.

The Beavers usually get winnowed out somewhere south of the policy meetings, but they can sometimes scramble up pretty high with this bustling activity before they get trapped.

The Beaver often compensates for lack of knowledge or lack of conviction by hustling around with his administrative details which seem to make a place for him at the table. It is often well to give him some stick to gnaw on, to keep his teeth out of the dam while the men do business.

Don't worry about him. But if his bustling gets in the way of your point you may want to give him something to do to keep his hot little claws occupied on the fringes of the subject. It's usually easily managed. He's good at going out of the room to check on some figures or to round up some information.

The Chameleon: Here is the soul of geniality. Before the meeting he goes in heavy for introductions. Wants to get everybody placed in his mind. Gives you nice, interested attention while you're talking to him . . . the same when the other fellow talks. But the uselessness of this man is his very good nature. He can see *everybody's* point of view. In fact, he will say, "Now I see your point, Ed, very clearly, and it's well taken, but . . . ah . . . Mike's got a point, too, when he says . . ."

Certainly. Everybody has a point, or he wouldn't even get in the door. But when you've won over Mr. Chameleon, you've won nothing. What he really wants is to get out of the room. He wishes he had never got up here in the first place. He's not in this league.

But you can't ignore him. He's a pretty good bellweather, and may be of use to you in seeing how the wind is blowing. He's quite sensitive, and his bobbing head will often point out to you where the biggest pile of chips is hidden.

The Old Horse: Lurking around in the room somewhere, at any level, there's apt to be a man in a baggy suit who seems so much at home that everyone either likes or respects him. That's the Old Horse. He probably won't carry the heaviest brass in the room but he's probably the happiest man present. That's the Old Horse.

Whatever is decided in the room, the Old Horse will

probably have to execute it. If there's a production consideration of any kind in the discussion, the Old Horse is there to tell them whether it can be done or not, and whether it's worth doing.

The Old Horse can afford to be relaxed and pleasant because a hundred times a day he sees evidence of his worth. So does everyone else, so he doesn't have to go around telling them. He won't tell *you* either. You've got to figure that out for yourself; and the sooner the better.

Identify also for your own protection and power the Sheep, the Fox and the Sleeping Possum.

6

Uncommon Sense in the Internal Meeting

Give Them a Score to Add Up

"GENTLEMEN, we *accomplished* something! Thanks."

Then sum it up, not just to show that you're running the meeting, but to send them out of the room taking big steps.

What men hate is the feeling of nonaccomplishment. It violates the basic human urge to be useful. Uselessness is the big killer. That's why the salesman is exhausted after a day when he makes no calls. But after a rugged eleven-hour day of continuous calls and hard selling, he's fresh as a daisy and ready for a big evening of strenuous relaxation.

Your people are the same way. If something was accomplished, spell it out so each man can chalk one up for himself. And while he's doing it, he chalks one up for you.

35

Credit

Give credit.

When a man comes up with a solution to a problem, let him see that his name is on that one. This is not so much for his sake as for yours.

If you can show the men in the meeting that any solution or effort they throw out on your roundtable will accrue to their score and that they can retain their identity with the idea, you'll find them glad to use your channel for their abilities. But if it looks as though you're going to put your own label all over it, they may just hold onto their wisdom until it has a chance to show up better.

Now obviously among adults you don't pass out gold stars. But there are ways of getting the credit across.

"Swell solution, Ed. I may want you to present that idea to the board in person. Be ready, will you?"

You don't want the credit. You want the job done, or you want the money or you want the promotion. You get that by letting Ed have the credit for everything he can do. Ultimately you get the credit anyway for inspiring Ed to such good performance. And the ability to inspire men is the highest priced commodity in today's market.

Should you ever doubt the motivating powers of credit, notice that when the assignments become more difficult than mere money can buy . . . the payoff is in credit. I doubt if you could have signed Sergeant Robert S. Kozeicky to a million-dollar contract to assault Hill 713 north of Salerno. But for $2.50 worth of Congressional Medal blue-ribbed silk . . . yes.

How would you meet this payroll if you had only money to offer?

President of the United States
Atomic research physicist
A man to spend fifteen years writing a dictionary
A typical hard-working minister

Men work for credit, not in the vulgar sense, but for the feeling that they are carrying their weight among men. In the case of the minister it is a more noble and eternal and subtle kind of credit. But in the case of the president, could you hire a competent man to serve anonymously . . . at what we pay him?

The Shut-out

In a meeting there is very apt to be an earnest, thorough, well-intending executive who is unwilling to dismiss the point after it is pretty much settled in everyone's mind. He wants to outline the procedure down to the last semicolon. He may temporarily have forgotten what level he's working on, and he pursues the matter through production, out into the packaging department and on down through the shipping department, and he may even get down to worrying about the pasting on of the label.

But if you let him run on, you're going to lose the respect, alertness and attention of the others at your meeting. You must stop him. It can be done. "Sam, you haven't time to worry about that. We'll get it handled."

Write in here two other ways to get this said, in language comfortable to yourself: go ahead—you'll find it more difficult than you think.

_____

_____

_____

_____

You Can Set the Pace

Open the meeting briskly, with staccato sentences and thoughts, briefly and firmly stated. Why? You will be able to set the pace of the meeting.

No man will wish to follow you with a dilatory, lethargic, wandering discussion. If the next man comes in with a negative pouting attitude, he will find it unfitting and ineffective in the face of the stimulating pace you have established. His opposition will become singularly unbecoming. Also the verbose, drawling, loose-thinking individual will hesitate to intrude any long-winded speeches after you have established this pace.

Have you ever watched a snappy little infantry platoon sergeant? A good one can bring a platoon to attention without even opening his mouth to issue the command. He snaps to attention himself with such compelling éclat that his platoon comes to attention by reflection, not by command.

You can set the pace for the meeting the same way.

Leaders Are Born . . . but More Often Made

There are natural-born leaders.

All natural-born leaders . . . and if you are one, you know it . . . should immediately put down this book.

Continuing now with only 99.9999 per cent of our readers, let's watch Uncle Sam handle the fact that there are not enough natural-born Napoleons, Pattons, Rommels, and MacArthurs to defend this or any country.

On two occasions in this century Uncle Sam has gone on the open market to buy leadership wholesale.

There weren't enough readymades to staff a full-scale police action against Estonia.

But the United States Army manufactured its own leaders in sufficient volume to command twenty-two million troops in two and one half wars.

To do this they found a substitute for "natural-born leadership." This substitute was so potent that when injected in large quantities into the veins of bespectacled, frightened, spindle-legged twenty-two-year-olds it stood up under the challenging stares of regulars who wore Panama-bleached leggings and a sleeve and a half of hashmarks and it outfaced the terrifying ka-whumps of 88mm. fire and the Banzai screech.

This substitute was called "prior planning."

A ninety-day wonder too young to remember wrap-around puttees could call a meeting of his platoon of veterans, and if he had prepared himself for the day's session on the operation of the .30-caliber Browning water-cooled M-1918, he could walk out of the barracks with the silent salute of respect and honor. And if he prepared himself before each subsequent meeting on only the subject which was scheduled, this prior planning habit became such a solid substitute for "natural-born leadership" that ultimately he could point to a hill full of Japanese Imperial Marines and two hundred Americans would surge forward against a curtain of flying lead and against every instinct of self-preservation ... because "the Old Man" (age twenty-two) said so.

In business this simple substitute is so little known and used that a practitioner of the old army rule of *prior planning* can fly to the top.

It is very simple. For that meeting tomorrow:

1) Know the subject.

2) Know the people.

3) Know how *you* want it to come out.

If you spend only a little time *today*—mastering the subject for *tomorrow*—you may find yourself effortlessly in charge of tomorrow's meeting.

If you know how you want it to come out, you may find the others give up by default. One man often becomes a majority . . . *if* he speaks.

If you spend a moment *today* deciding what objections will be raised and by *whom*, you will have good answers for them by tomorrow.

What will Higgins' attitude be? Will Miller oppose this? On what grounds? How can I convert him? passify him? override him? Or perhaps Higgins is right.

How Far Will You Go?

A most important part of this prior planning is to study your*self* to see how far *you* are willing to go to maintain your point. The others will probably not have decided what their own limits-of-action are. If you know what you are willing to settle for . . . or how far *you* are willing to go for your objectives, you will probably have your way.

Decide: Am I willing to lose the contract if the price is under $200 per unit?

If no one will execute my proposal, am I willing to say, "All right, gentlemen, if you'll give me the authority and the money, I'll get it done myself."

If they try to beat me down to a force of seven men to do a certain job, will I accept the assignment on that basis or do I draw the line at eight?

If the price goes above $200 per unit, am I willing to do without it?

If you enter the room with your own mind made up on these questions, you'll usually have the advantage over others who plan to arrive at these decisions after they get to the meeting.

Brilliant generals or executives or football coaches know before the contest how much they are willing to expend for a given objective. Good traders know before the dicker begins what figures they are willing to pay if necessary. But the majority do not . . . which is why auctions can thrive. Auctions are conferences.

A still further advantage to this prior planning is the

fact that the mere act of preparing and deciding upon one's own limits often makes it unnecessary to reach this showdown point; because a little prior planning often reveals alternatives which you can propose to head off the showdown.

Example: In the case of the ten men you requested for a certain job, perhaps management will say to you, "We'd be glad to give you ten men, but there are only seven available." Your prior planning *today* anticipates such a reply and by tomorrow perhaps you can show them where three more men can be had. You can call their bluff . . . because you're prepared. More on this subject later from another angle.

7

Imagination in the Conference

When General MacArthur was commandant at West Point he called meetings of his staff to announce new policies. When he particularly did not wish much discussion, the story is told that instead of calling his meeting at the typical times, like 1:00 P.M. or 4:00 P.M. or 9:00 A.M., he would announce the meeting for 5:15 P.M., or, as he envisioned it, just a little before dinner. Hungry, tired men expected home for dinner do not harangue very long.

In this same direction many executives are now making more use of the day and at the same time dramatizing to their people the importance of time by ignoring the standard time segments. It is customary to set the time for a conference on the hour or the half hour or occasionally the quarter hour. But frequently it makes more sense to call the meeing for 10:20 or 10:55.

This is being done increasingly. Time is time, regardless of nice symmetry on the face of your watch. Some

men carry it much further, scheduling meetings for
eighteen minutes after ten.

Perhaps this suggests to you a "character." Definitely
it would strike a sour note in the hands of some men.
But a certain rubber tire executive for whom we have
high regard carries it off so well that we find ourselves
trying to help save his time. He has been overheard to
say over the phone, "Yes, I want very much to see you,
Sam. Could you meet me twelve or thirteen minutes after
three? Sounds funny, I know, but I want all the time I
can get with you and I have another commitment later."

The harried, high-pressure executive is becoming a
caricature. "I haven't got much time" has become the
mark of inefficiency, so you don't usually say it. But if
you set the time for twelve after three, you've made it
plainer than words.

Making allies of the junior members of a conference
is good long-term business. Leo Rosencrans, an extremely
skillful salesman, was attempting to sell an $80,000 in-
dustrial motion picture to the firm of Beaumont & Hoh-
man. At the preliminary meeting a young man named
J. F. Turk was very much the junior-most executive
present on the buyer's side. After Mr. Rosencrans had
concluded his presentation the president asked for opinions from each of his men.

Most of them spoke favorably about the product being
offered. Some quibbled at the price. Others found a few
objections to it. Young Turk was the last one asked. He
didn't know enough about the product to venture much

of an opinion. Yet he didn't want to be blandly opinionless. So he said, "It seems like a good proposal to me. However, I think Mr. Rosencrans is in error about the tonnage of stainless steel produced this year in Pittsburgh."

Now the man to watch is not Turk, but Rosencrans. The meeting was concluded, deferring final action until a later meeting. In the interim Turk received a letter from Rosencrans:

> Dear Mr. Turk:
>
> I have had time to check on the point you raised. I find that my figures *are* doubtful. Does your comment mean that you have the correct figures? I would appreciate it if you would bring them to the next meeting.
>
> Sincerely yours,

When the next meeting took place young Turk had dug up correct figures, at some trouble to himself. He therefore already had an investment of time in Rosencrans's project. You don't like to throw away an investment.

Rosencrans, being a major figure in the industry, could have brushed off the minor matter; but he knew that an ambitious young man with a point to make and a career to build can puncture a lot of big balloons.

> *Postscript:* J. F. Turk has since taken over a big job at Beaumont & Hohman, which will make him one of the country's large buyers of motion picture film.

Occasionally it is wise to have the other men in the room make your points for you. John Gardiner was sales manager for a large gasoline and oil company. The firm was having trouble getting its dealers to follow a standard method for handling customers. Gardiner called in his dealers and asked them to formulate a policy for the handling of every customer who drove into one of the company's gas stations. In the meeting room he had a large blackboard. In his pocket he had an eight-point list of how he wanted each customer to be handled. But he left the list in his pocket.

He said, "Now I'd like you dealers to formulate the company policy for handling every customer who drives in. What should be our first step?"

By drawing replies from his dealers, by letting the dealers argue down the weak suggestions themselves and by occasionally pointing out repetitious suggestions, he wound up with eight points written on the blackboard. They were the eight points which were on the card in his pocket. However, they were in a slightly different order.

Gardiner now asked the men, "Take a second look at the importance of the eight points on the board. Should any of the steps for handling a customer be arranged in a different sequence?"

The meeting ended at 3:30 in the afternoon. Gardiner said, "The eight steps which we have decided upon here this afternoon will henceforth be the policy of this company in handling customers."

Gardiner's company experienced no more difficulty in getting its dealers to carry out the company policy.

Sometimes meetings bog down in heated argument. As the argument lengthens, the perspectives of the men narrow until by 4:00 P.M. they are dissecting commas with a scalpel. Frequently it is apparent to someone in the room that if you could get the men back into a state of mind where they view the broad picture in proper perspective, a solution could be reached. But given a group of men who have been ground down to a myopic state, how can you lift them back up so they see things the way they did at 9:00 A.M.? How can you suddenly make them see the problem at hand in relation to the company welfare, and the company welfare in relation to the nation and the world, and in relation to their own reason for being?

George Franklin had a way of doing this. He ripped a page out of a book which belonged to his son, and he carried it in his wallet. It was a page from Mr. F. Hoyle's book, *The Nature of the Universe.*

Occasionally when a meeting degenerated to splitting semicolons, George Franklin pulled this wrinkled page out of his wallet and grinned. He said, "Gentlemen, I'd like to read you a paragraph—with a few changes—which is pertinent to this matter. I think it will solve our problem here today."

The men were usually impatient at this diversion and did not listen very carefully at first. But as Franklin read on they were apt to lean forward attentively and the walls of the room moved back to give a man a wider view of the relative importance of things.

Here is the section he read:

> Once a photograph of the Earth,* taken from outside, is available, we shall, in an emotional sense, acquire an additional dimension. The common idea of motion is an essentially two-dimensional idea. It concerns only transportation from one place on the surface of the Earth to another. How many of us realize that but for a few miles of atmosphere above our heads we should be frozen hard as a board every night? Apart from the petty motion of the airplane, motion upward as yet means nothing to us. But once let the possibility of outward motion become as clear to the average man at a football match as it is to the scientist in his laboratory, once let the sheer isolation of the Earth become plain to every man whatever his nationality or creed, and a new idea as powerful as any in history will be let loose. And I think this not too distant development may well be for good, as it must increasingly have the effect of exposing the futility of such puny concerns as our international wars.

"Now suppose we make a plan of how the sun and planets are arranged . . . to see how our concerns fit in the scheme of things. 'In our plan let us represent the Sun as a ball six inches in diameter. . . . Now how far away are the planets from our ball? . . . Mercury is seven yards

---

*Now widely available, of course. Whether the initial shock of seeing such photographs has led to any permanent attitude change is a matter for debate.

away, Venus thirteen, the Earth eighteen, Mars twenty-seven, Jupiter ninety, Saturn one hundred seventy. Uranus is three hundred and fifty, or 3½ football fields away. Pluto is just less than a half mile away.' Now on this scale what size model do we use to represent the Earth? We would find the smallest speck of dust that we could pick up on the point of a damp needle. Now suppose you could be transported to a position in the Universe where you could look at these units in their . . ."

When George Franklin gets that far a new perspective has usually lightened the room.

Many a hassle results from the effort to set standards and define terms. You've seen it.

What will we consider an acceptable product? What is a satisfactory sales quota? What do you mean when you say "reasonable performance"? What kind of conduct on the part of another nation shall we consider peaceful?

In such an argument the verbiage can drown the main project before it even gets off the ground. The same word can mean something different to everyone at the table. There is suddenly a crying need for a simple specific.

Ben Fairless, later head of U.S. Steel, had such a situation. When he was working for the Central Steel Company the army was complaining about faults in the steel. Fairless was assigned to work with the army and reach an agreement with them about what would be the standard.

For this purpose he had a meeting with the army inspectors. There were many ways he could have proceeded to set a standard. The most obvious, if the most tiresome and expensive, would have been to have the army engineers draw up a thick docket of specifications while his own engineers drew up another. Then with these two documents before them they could have sat down and melded the two into a single standard for acceptable steel. It probably could have been accomplished in a week or two, and maybe four or five meetings.

But while such alternatives were being discussed, Fairless said, "Gentlemen, I think I have an idea you'll like better."

He reached over to the ashtray and picked out of it a stray paper clip which one of the inspectors had just thrown away.

He bent the paper clip back and forth until it broke in half. He handed one half to the chief army inspector and kept one half himself. "If any steel has pits big enough for us to poke this clip in," Fairless said easily, "let's agree it's faulty."

The army was delighted at the clear-cut simplicity. The argument was over. A lot of time and sweat and adrenalin had been saved.

8

Some Masters of the Conference

THE MEN who win conferences regularly can't tell you how they do it. It's second nature, reflex. And their methods are as various as the men. But they go through the basic common-sense reasoning that applies to anyone, even though subconsciously. It's become automatic. Let's watch a few of the masters in action.

Often a conference can be best handled by laying the disadvantages of two alternatives clearly on the table and letting the people select their own course of action.

General Eisenhower told the story of a conference—one involving several thousand people.

Five United States senators had come to his command post immediately after he had received a telegram explaining that a newspaper article was charging poor food and housing and handling of men at Camp Lucky Strike.

Eisenhower knew that no such condition should exist if orders were being carried out, and he wished to investigate in person immediately.

51

He therefore invited the five senators to accompany him on this inspection trip in his plane.

It was a quick two-hour trip. The general and the senators inspected the camp. They found the food was fine. There was some justification for complaint in that the camp physicians had ordered no seasoning be allowed, considering it damaging to these troops who had just undergone periods of starvation in prison camps and in combat. Eisenhower did not think he should overrule the doctors on this point.

The real basis of complaint to be found was the length of time the men had to wait in this camp for transportation back to the States. They could see ships leaving the harbor practically empty, and it looked to them like mishandling. What they didn't know was that these ships were freighters with no drinking water and sanitary provisions for large numbers of troops, nor bunks.

Eisenhower and the senators walked back to the plane, the inspection completed. By then thousands of soldiers had gathered near the ship to get a look at the commanding general. Some soldiers had rigged up a microphone and a PA system, and they asked the general to say a few words.

Ike looked at the crowd of men who had endured suffering beyond imagination and he could think of nothing to say to them at the moment that would be significant. But suddenly he wished very much for some way to get them all home quickly. And at that moment a plan came to him which he would not have considered under other conditions.

He took the microphone, and after a brief greeting he said, "There are two ways we can get you home. The first is to load on every returning troop ship the maximum number for which it was designed. Or—since submarines are no longer a menace—we could put on each troop ship twice the number of men she's designed for. You understand this would mean that you would be very crowded, and one man would have to sleep in the daytime so another soldier could have his bunk at night. Which of the two plans would you prefer?"

A roar of voices went up which obviously meant: the latter.

When the roar died down General Ike said, "Very well, that's the way we shall do it. But I must warn you men that there are five United States senators accompanying me today. Consequently when you get home it will do you no good to write letters to the papers or your senators complaining about overcrowding on the ships. Remember, you made the choice."

An enormous laugh filled the field and there was no doubt that they would live with their choice happily. But if such a system had been instituted in a routine manner, there could have been much disapproval.

In certain other kinds of situations a man can blast his way out of a tough spot in a conference by using the extra bald truth, coupled with a slight grin. You have to know what you're doing. But it works.

In the 1934 World Series between the Cardinals and

the Tigers, Bill Delancey, the Cardinals' catcher, got into trouble with Judge Kenesaw Mountain Landis, the commissioner.

During the Series three strikes were called on Delancey by Umpire Brick Owens. Delancey thought it was a bad call, and he exploded, "Why you ——— ——— blind so-and-so! Can't you see the ball?"

Owens thought this was a too-personal question. It was somehow reported to Judge Landis who summoned Delancey to his room.

Delancey reported in. Landis kept him standing in front of him. He said, "Young man, what did you say to Mr. Owens after the third strike was called on you today?"

A wounded, puzzled look came over Delancey's face as he turned up his palms. "Why, Judge, all I said was, 'Why you ——— ——— blind so-and-so! Can't you see the ball?' Just a simple question, that's all. Is there any harm in that?"

Judge Landis swiveled his chair toward the window, covered his mouth with a long, bony hand and coughed. "That will be all, Delancey," he said.

Often the best way to win a conference is by action. John Patterson of the National Cash Register Company invited all his salesmen into Dayton, Ohio, for a big meeting in which he called for a large increase in sales for the coming year. The meeting was held in the company dining room. Patterson called for an increase which would step the whole operation up to an entirely new level.

However, as he watched his salesmen listening, he could see they were not sparking to his new program. They listened in the relaxed manner of men who are listening to a challenge too enormous to be taken seriously.

Patterson interrupted his remarks at two o'clock in the afternoon and said, "Gentlemen, I am apparently putting this badly. We will adjourn immediately and reconvene here at breakfast tomorrow morning at nine. At that time I will have found a more persuasive way to prove to you that these objectives are entirely attainable."

The salesmen were surprised, not only that Patterson had adjourned the meeting, but that he had been so perceptive as to sense from the platform exactly how they felt. However, they left the dining hall.

One of Patterson's aides said, "Mr. Patterson, why did you stop?"

"Because I could see the men felt the objective was too big to be accomplished. They weren't taking me seriously. We will prove to them by tomorrow morning that anything is possible."

"How?"

"You're going to do it. I want you to begin now. When these men return to this dining room tomorrow morning for breakfast, I want the dining room to have completely disappeared. I want not one stick or stone of this building to remain. And I want grass to be growing here as though there never was any building here."

"But how . . ."

"Anything can be done."

"Yes, Mr. Patterson."

Men who worked close to Patterson knew he meant what he said, that he was not joking.

Three demolition companies arrived that afternoon and began tearing down and hauling away the dining room.

An excavation company was commissioned to start hauling in dirt to fill in the basement. While the excavation people worked a farmer's pasture was quickly leased. Hay mowers moved over the pasture cutting down the grass. After the hay mowers, a battery of lawn mowers moved over the pasture. After the lawn mowers a platoon of landscape gardeners arrived at the pasture and began cutting the pasture into long strips of sod. Darkness set in. Twenty automobiles were lined up beside the pasture with their headlights playing over it. The landscape gardeners rolled up the sod in great carpetlike strips which were loaded on trucks.

At the site of the dining hall, and by the headlights of the trucks, the strips of sod were laid down and watered.

A local horticulturist delivered two hundred potted geraniums just after midnight. By daybreak the last of the geraniums was transplanted in a star-shaped pattern in the middle of the grassed-over area.

At breakfast time a bewildered sales force of the National Cash Register Company wandered over the grounds looking for the dining hall. Finally they converged around the geranium bed. John Patterson stood there.

"It was worth it to make my point, gentlemen. You see anything . . . I mean *anything* . . . can be done."

In certain situations pure, austere presumption wins the conference.

The Cunard Line, which operated the great fleet of passenger vessels whose names ended in the letters "ia" (the *Coronia*, the *Franconia*) wanted to name its greatest ship the *Queen Victoria*.

Accordingly their representative sought audience with King George V. After the exchange of formalities, the spokesman for the steamship line said, "Sir, we would like your permission to name our latest vessel for England's greatest queen. We . . ."

But the King interrupted, smiling pleasantly. "The Queen will be very pleased, gentlemen."

Hence the *Queen Victoria* became the *Queen Mary*.

The toughest conferences can be won decisively if you can manage a proposal so dramatically fair that the justice of it flashes to everyone around the table. Such solutions are not easy to come by in complex affairs. But if you have one, use it.

Judge Seth Pease was a circuit judge in the frontier
stage of Ohio's development. Many of his best decisions
were rendered outside of formal court, for he was often
asked to arbitrate disputes which the contestants did not
wish to bring to formal litigation.

Tow frontiersmen, Harter and Murphy, were in hot
dispute over a tract of land. Each had title to half the
tract, but they could not decide where the boundary line
was.

Pease listened to the argument from both principals
and also from their surveyors and the neighbors. He finally agreed to arbitrate the argument providing both
Murphy and Harter were willing. They were.

Pease thought it over for two days, and then after
church on Sunday morning he announced his decision.
"Murphy, you will draw the boundary line which you
believe will exactly bisect the tract."

Murphy smiled. "Yes, *sir!*"

"And then," continued Seth Pease, "Harter will have
first choice which half he wants."

Smiles broke among the bystanders. Justice is a great
settler of questions at any conference table.

Nothing so quickly and effectively clears the smoke
in a tense conference room as a blast of whimsy.

In a tense, high-level sales policy conference in Pitts-
field, the room was split in half over the argument:
Shall the most convenient production level of the factory govern the sales quotas for company salesmen? Or,

shall the indicated capacity of the market and the company's previous history of percentage participation be the formula for governing the salesmen's annual quotas?

It's a basic argument as old as mass production, and it's one that will not be solved tomorrow. Sales executives believe that you start with the reasonable possibilities of the market, and tell the factory to produce accordingly. Production executives usually feel that you set a level of production at which your factory can produce the most competitive price and quality, then order your sales force to sell this output.

In this particular argument the sales chief and the production chief were seated side by side. In the course of making his points the production chief sent out of the room for some figures to prove his point. A junior executive brought in the figures which were cited by Mr. Production.

The figures were challenged by the sales vice president who in turn sent out of the room for something. His secretary soon returned, handed him a slip of paper and departed. The sales manager continued his argumentation, but made no reference to the figures nor to the slip of paper which he held shielded in his cupped hand.

As the argument intensified the production chief kept nervously eyeing the slip of paper in the sales manager's hand. Finally he exploded, "Well, you still haven't said anything to answer my figures!" He glared at the cupped hand of the sales manager.

The sales manager grinned a little. "How could I?" he asked.

And he turned his hand so that the belligerent one could read the slip of paper. The production chief burst into a roaring laugh, grabbed the slip and slid it out on the table where all could laugh.

It said, "Bring home a loaf of bread."

Production and sales went out of the room slapping each other on the back. The problem wasn't solved. But there was a sudden mutually comforting re-recognition of the fact that the opposition was after all just a human man. Sales ceased to be Mr. A. W. Sales and became a husband, father . . . a person. Production ceased to be a bull-headed worm gear with a time-study mind, and became a regular guy who also had enough kids and domestic life to laugh at the note.

Somehow it suddenly becomes easy to live and let live with a man whose executive shield drops for an instant. The sales manager knew this. He wouldn't have had to uncover the slip.

Gerald Van Schoor is often in a defensive type conference. He is a home office technical expert on his company's special kind of thermal piping. Occasionally a customer will challenge the performance of the product after installation. This happens in any business. It becomes Van Schoor's job to go and inspect the installation of the product. If it is not correctly installed by the user he must point this out to the customer, so that an equitable solution can be reached about sharing the cost of repairing the installation.

He is very successful at this principally because of his complete fairness. But in addition he has developed one tactic which helps him immensely. He says, "When you're alone, and you're talking to a group of four or more men, always arrange to sit between them. Split them two and two, and sit in the middle. Do not let the four men sit opposite you on one side of the table to face you like a board of inquisition. They gather too much support from each other, and the very physical arrangement actually sharpens the lines of contest. It's too much like choosing up sides; and even if a man wants to agree with your reasoning, it goes too much against the physical alignment. It's as though he were crossing the table. But if he's sitting beside you, it's very easy for him to express his honest agreement with you."

In a conference, much of the art of winning is allowing the other man to retain his self-respect.

The height of this art was employed by Richard Plover in a dicker for the use of a boar. Plover was a new farmer. He had changed from manufacturing to running two large farms, and he knew that his newness sometimes subjected him to higher prices than the usual.

He knew the exact strain of boar he wished to use, and he even knew the exact boar he wanted. It belonged to James Rand.

Plover first checked to see what was the going rate for rental on a boar of such quality. It was $2.50 per sow.

He drove to Rand's farm and began negotiations. They

got as far as price. Rand quoted five dollars per sow.

Plover did not reply. He stood there scratching his chin for fully two minutes. Finally, "Seems just a bit high," he said.

Rand did not reply. He stood silent, lighting his pipe. The silence built up. Finally he said, "Uh . . . did you say you'd come for the boar in your truck?"

Plover agreed instantly. "Oh, yes. I forgot to say, we'll come for the boar."

Rand said, "We could do it for four dollars."

Plover did not reply. He scratched his chin, removed his hat, studied the inside of it, put it back on his head. Then he drew his fist across his chin and held quiet.

Rand said, "Uh . . . did you say you'd bring the boar back in your truck?"

Plover quickly agreed, "Yes, I forgot to say, we'll bring the boar back, too."

Rand said, "In that case three dollars will cover it."

Plover did not reply. He studied his boots, removed a tuft of grass that was clinging to his heel. He took off his hat, ran his hands through his hair, replaced his hat and kept quiet.

Rand said, "Uh . . . you say you'd furnish feed and return him before Monday."

Plover came alert. "I forgot to say, we'll furnish feed and return him by Sunday night, eight o'clock sharp."

Rand said, "I guess we could do it for $2.50 a head."

Plover let down the ramp of his truck. Rand walked to the boar pen. Respect existed between both men.

This same problem of price or conditions of contract

takes place in industry and commerce a million times a day at all levels. The principles remain the same. Let the other man save face.

Boldness wins in a conference.

During one of this country's minor financial panics, the banks were going to close down Augustus Swift, the meat packer.

Twelve banks found that they were creditors of Swift's. And the strong suspicion grew on them that Swift was seriously overextended. Each bank assumed that it was the major creditor, and they agreed to call Swift before them in joint meeting to demand a few explanations and immediate payment.

Swift *was* in trouble, and he was busy in a critical struggle to keep his doors open. He was in fact just leaving for the East to seek more credit when the summons arrived. But he knew he would have to defer his trip to attend this meeting. He sat down at his desk and thought out what he would say to them.

When he arrived at the meeting he had no briefcase, no accompanying assistants or accountants, just a single sheet of paper.

The apparent chairman of the group of bankers cleared his throat and began a circuitously polite approach to the embarrassing subject. But Swift interrupted. "Gentlemen, if I may, I'll speak first. I'm glad of this opportunity, as I was going to seek you out anyway." There was some visible relief around the table, but that was followed by a gasp because Swift said, "You see I'm applying for a loan extension from each of you." Eyebrows went up. "And in addition I will require additional loans from each of you by about double my present notes."

It takes time to muster an answer for such effrontery. But Swift drew the sheet of paper from his pocket. "I thought it would be considerate of me to let you all know how much capital the others have advanced me."

He read the figures, and each banker saw that he was not the major creditor, that any division of assets would have to divide out rather thin around the table. "I believe all of our best interests lie in keeping this ship afloat." Swift reached for his hat.

The Swift Company is very much in business today.

9

Let's Start

ONE OF THE most memorable conferences we have attended in recent years took place in a second-floor hallway of a small but brisk and prosperous company engaged in the production of motion pictures in the Midwest. The president and owner of the business sent word to the studio manager that he would like to have an oversized table, which was resting at the head of the stairway, brought down to the first floor. The conference resulted when four employees went upstairs to bring down the table. Eyeing the table and the stairwell opening, it was apparent that a certain amount of maneuvering would be necessary.

One of the conferees suggested that the simplest method of arriving at the objective would be to remove the legs from the table. There were certain objections to this method of attack. Admittedly, it would be the safer course, but it seemed like a lot of work, when the table might fit anyway; besides, that would take time and the table was needed right away.

Idea number two proposed measuring the width of the table and the size of the opening, thus eliminating guesswork regarding the clearance. This nearly carried the day until someone suggested that it wouldn't really prove anything, since the table could be turned on its side and that would be a different dimension. It was pointed out that this dimension, too, could be measured. However, the dissenter argued that the angle at which the table was held in relation to the staircase would alter the clearance and therefore no sensible measurements could be taken; besides, no one knew where to find a ruler in a hurry.

Meanwhile, the owner, whose order had started the conference, had become impatient for the table. He joined the conference.

The conferees explained the considerations that had thus far been under discussion. The owner listened with labored restraint. Then he said, "All right, now let's do it my way."

"What way is that?"

"Let's start." Whereupon everyone took hold of a corner and maneuvered the table down the stairway.

Now, if this seems to you to be a flippant and inconsequential instance of resolving a conference, you have not attended many. Every day across this broad land, hundreds of business conferences become ensnarled in the same kind of foolish dilemmas as we have cited here. It should be significant to you that it was the *owner* of the business who broke up this particular conference with the suggestion to start.

One of the more significant things to remember about the conference is that it would never have been called if someone had had the courage to go ahead without it.

Getting started is often a very uncomfortable procedure. People are likely to procrastinate about it and a conference all too often becomes group procrastination. More and more reasons are advanced for proceeding with caution because every man is born with an innate premonition of disaster. It takes very little imagination to anticipate the dire consequences of any action.

But it takes leadership and a certain amount of enthusiasm to point out and sell the possible good reactions that can result from a definite course of action. Usually, any course at all can be steered down the road to success. The important thing is to take that highly overrated and greatly feared first step.

In the conference the man who says, "Let's start. I'll do so and so, you do so and so," is the man whose opinion will be sought for the next conference.

Perhaps you're thinking, "That's fine, but if I'm the one who starts something, what do I do if it doesn't work out?" The answer to this is, if you start something see that it does work out. Keep your original enthusiasm alive. That will almost inevitably forestall failure.

And what if it doesn't?

Well, remember the thing they pay for in America is risk. If you won't take it, you won't make it.

If you're the man who says, "Let's start," and if your timing is correct, make no mistake about it, you've elected yourself captain. If you can be identified as the man who came forward with a plan of action, you have to a degree absolved the others of a responsibility. No one will remember whose idea it was if the action succeeds, everyone will remember if it fails. That's why there was a conference. Somebody wanted to shift that responsibility.

We know of an advertising agency that is experiencing some very difficult times. It was once a strong organization. Today it is headed for failure. The management is aware of the difficulty but is unable to put its finger on the source.

To an outsider who has occasion to join the people of this agency in conference, the reason is quite apparent. An all too common form of corporate paralysis has seized this group. It has too many conferences and they last interminably. That in itself is not an insurmountable difficulty, but an observer soon notes that ideas are slow in coming to this table. When they do come they are interjected timidly and without conviction. No one seems to want to be identified with a course of action. It takes considerable time to arrive at a decision and that never happens until all responsibility for the decision has been obliterated. Everyone leaves the meeting confident that if things don't work out, no one can point the finger at him.

This burying of responsibility in the anonymity of the conference is a serious thing and management should fear it like the plague. It is hard to recognize. What seems to be a productive meeting of the minds can easily be, in reality, skilled ball passing or mass cowardice. If it becomes a habit it brings disaster.

First of all, such timidity deprives the organization of the best thinking of its men. They're doing the thinking all right, they just aren't expressing their thoughts.

Decisions reached without identity are likely to be the least common denominator of all the minds at work. If no ONE can be identified with a course of action, no ONE is responsible for it and no one is pushing it to successful conclusion. Let that sort of thing accumulate for a few years and there will be space to let.

If you recognize such a situation in your company don't try to correct it unless you're very high up in its counsels. There is always good reason when thinking men maneuver for anonymity. Chances are the company where such a situation exists isn't going any place and you'd be better off out of it.

Now if you find yourself thinking back over some of the more recent conferences that have taken place in your circle, and if you're saying, "Why, that's just what they're doing at our place," be careful. We said earlier, the symptoms we have described are difficult to recognize. Most conferees are cautious. Don't get that mixed up with cowardice. It's a matter of degree and it takes careful observation to tell which is which. Your best guide is the outcome of the conference. If a clear-cut decision is reached, or if a definite course of action is decided upon and assignments made, chances are the situation we've been talking about has not developed, at least not in its dangerous, crippling form. Identity is the key to it. If one man or a small group of men emerge with the responsibility to direct a course of action then all is well.

Now for a moment let's assume that you have taken this chapter to heart. You've attended a conference and got your mouth open. You said, "Let's start"; and now you find yourself carrying the ball.

This authority will involve many conferences with other people—conferences that you will call—conferences that you will run. Now it's an entirely different game you're in. You're not functioning with the staff anymore, you're on the line, in charge of a campaign.

You can make a lot of mistakes, and you're quite aware of it. We'd like to point out here a few of the less obvious errors—the kind that might not occur to you.

Let us presume that you're entirely competent to work with your subordinates and your equals to lead the attack. Where you are likely to be on less familiar ground is with your superiors . . . the people who put this authority in your hands in the first place.

An all too common error at this stage is the tendency some of us have to go back to the seat of power for reassurance. Perhaps an illustration will bring out the point.

You work for an applicance manufacturer. The competition just announced its new models and they feature a magnetic door latch which has your big brass in a tizzy. Your new models are ready but not yet announced, and you have no such flashy gimmick with which to dazzle the public.

That's why the big conference was called. You suggested calling in a clever engineering firm of your acquaintance because you were sure they could come up with a magnetic door latch as good as the competition's, overnight. That broke up the conference. You were authorized to go ahead.

You called a conference with your own design engineers to determine the restrictions (size, space, weight, cost, function) that you would have to impose on your clever engineering friends. You called conferences with your company's production men, sales department, legal department and all the rest and you now can talk intelligently with your outside engineering consultants. All this is routine, obvious action and within your authority.

Now you are sitting across the table from your consultants. They've listened to your story and right then and there sketched a rough drawing of a door latch which they think might meet the need.

What do you do now? Call a conference of the big brass and show them the rough sketch? Maybe even present your engineering friends and let them explain their idea? This would relieve you of making a commitment of time and money. It would be sane and safe.

It would probably also make you a permanent assistant to the assistant.

Now this is the point: if you are going to be an executive you must begin to act like one. Don't call that conference of the big brass. Take the risk. That's what you were authorized to do. Commit your company to pay the bill for developing the idea that is now just a rough sketch. Do even more. Tell your engineering brains to cook up several other alternative ideas, just in case this one doesn't work out. You won't have accomplished anything until you bring in a door latch that meets the need. So damn the torpedoes, get the door latch; then call in the big brass.

So much for the example. The point is, when you've been given the opportunity, don't stand around savoring it. Don't try to use it to establish better communications with the big boys. Even if you think there'll be a chance to show what a clever boy you are, and probably there will be chances, don't go back to brass until your mission is accomplished, or until you absolutely need further authority to accomplish it.

If this seems an obvious course, hardly worth all the space we have devoted to it, realize that one of the most difficult things a man on the way up has to get used to is this exercise of new authority. A lot of mistakes have been made by young men assuming too much authority, of course. But it takes a rather stupid young man to make that mistake and we presume you are mature enough not to make it.

The more common and more subtle error is the one we have just described, that of not acting like an executive when you have been given the right.

To conclude, the young man going somewhere in the company is the one who is willing to say "Let's start."

Have in mind a plan of action, even if it's only a logical first step. Then get behind that plan and make it work. Seize the authority and turn it into opportunity.

Most often authority is not something you're given; it's something you take.

And don't forget: time spent in conference is overhead. Time spent in executing decisions of the conference is productive.

10

Things to Look for When You Hire a Management

PERHAPS, as you've been digesting these pages, you've been saying to yourself, "That might be good advice for the big shots, but if I tried some of the things they've been talking about I'd find myself out in the street."

If that's your attitude, what we have to say now could be important.

When you were hired, do you remember the questions they asked you? Remember the interviews? How you got your suit pressed special? The store-bought shine you went out of your way to get? Remember how you tried to anticipate their questions so you'd be ready with the right answers?

Now then, what questions did *you* ask? Did you ask for a financial statement of the company covering the past five years? Did you inquire what changes were contemplated in the product to meet competition? Did you ask what experience the president of the company had to warrant his high place? Did you check on the company's credit, its capital structure, the ownership of its stock?

Did it not occur to you that if the company were entitled to this kind of information about you, you in turn were entitled to know as much about the company?

After all, in accepting the job, you did some hiring too. You, in effect, hired a management to build a future for you.

Every sound management recognizes this. Such management is as concerned about its employees as it is about its customers. After all, customers it can get; good, loyal, productive employees have to be made—and that's expensive.

Now maybe you're saying, "That's all very well, I know how true it is, but you try telling it to Mr. Blusterfuss." If you're saying something like that, perhaps it's time you took a good long look at Mr. B and all the little b's around him.

Many learned tomes have been written, principally by people with doctors' degrees or masters' degrees working on their doctors' theses, having to do with the history of American business management. These point out with great elaborateness what any alert young businessman has already observed for himself. Namely, that the owners of today's businesses seldom manage them. The owners hire professionals to run the outfits.

While this is a pretty safe generalization and worth perhaps several books to explain how the sons of the founders all turned out to be playboys and are incapable of running the old man's shop, there are many, many notable exceptions. New businesses are being founded every day and the owners are very much the managers.

Generally, however, as a business thrives and grows larger and older the original management retires or dies, or the capital requirements are such that the money lenders want a watchdog on the scene. Either way, control passes to an employee who is not an owner, or at least not *the* owner.

What sort of man this manager will be at any given moment depends in great measure on what the company's needs are at the time he's appointed. Thus, if the problem is one of increasing the capitalization he'll most likely be a banker. If sales are the problem, he'll be a man of proven sales-organizing ability. If the company's in financial straits, he'll probably be a lawyer or high-level accountant.

And as the company's needs change, very often the managerial background will change with them. The banker, who has placed the company in a very good capital position, becomes chairman of the board and if, meanwhile, the new capitalization has increased production facilities to where sales are the problem, then the new manager is likely to be a sales organizer, and so on.

What has all this to do with the business conference? Well, just a moment, we're coming to that.

Now as the managements change to meet the needs as we have outlined above, several obvious things happen. First of all the new management doesn't know the trimetal bearings on the F 452-11 model from the door hinge.

The new management can be depended upon to make

an honest effort to learn, but this will be unsuccessful since it is unimportant. A "technical man" (all men who understand such things the new management calls "technical men") can be hired to look after that end of the business. This lack of knowledge of the production phase of the business is the first and biggest departure from the company's traditional organization. The founder of the business knew all about trimetal bearings, he probably invented them, and everybody around *him* knew all about them, too.

The new management, knowing how vulnerable it is because of this mechanical ignorance, will create a technical or engineering department. It will put the best man it can find at the head of this operation and will elevate him to the status of vice president. This engineering vice president will not necessarily or even usually be a very good engineer. He will, however, know where and how to hire good engineers, and he will be able to interpret their findings to the management in such a way that he guides them effectively.

Now the new management's attitude toward the engineering department will be that it is well handled, since the man in charge is being paid $200,000 a year. Outside of conferences and some gestures for appearance' sake, the management ceases to be interested in the engineering department as long as there are no obvious problems, and concerns itself with the real business at hand which is, let us say, getting the company into a strong financial position.

Similarly, the new management has had little experience in handling large numbers of industrial employees. A man can be hired to take care of this too. If a particularly large number of people is involved this man will receive the title "Vice President, Personnel." Otherwise, he will simply be the "manager of our personnel department." In either case he will be expected to handle the employees completely.

The banker-type management is not likely to know much about selling, so there will be a vice president in charge of sales, as well as a sales manager. These two positions will have the highest rate of turnover during difficult times.

Now the banker-type management is likely to have had considerable experience with accounting methods, and in its opinion this is really the most important end of the business since it is here that profit and loss show up and can be controlled. A good and trusted friend from a previous connection is most likely to be appointed comptroller of the company under the banker management. This comptroller will be seen in the company of the president more than anyone else. When any decision has to be made in other departments, this comptroller person is likely to be consulted, even though he is not even remotely concerned. His influence will be felt all down the line. His assistants will have more weight than the assistants from other departments. Before long everyone who works for the company will be aware of this influence and will adjust accordingly.

Now let's suppose the banker-type management serves its purpose by putting the company in a sound financial position and the time comes around for another change.

The trustees are well aware that the capital structure is now secure, but they're getting a little itchy about sales. Who will the new manager be? A sales organizer, of course.

This man, whom we will call Lew for now, has considerably more interest in the engineering department. He's been selling the product and knows what they say about it in the field. He knows what changes are needed to bring it up to the competition. The engineering vice president suddenly finds himself with a more powerful voice. His assistants have more powerful voices.

The sales-type manager knows something of the effectiveness of advertising, so the advertising manager finds himself attending the major conferences. His opinions, too, are sought and respected.

But the comptroller? Well, he's put back on his stool to report once a month or so on the bank balance. Lew feels that the accountants only add up the results, never contribute to them. As for the bankers, well, Lew figures if he sells the stuff the company'll make profits and if profits are being made any banker will loan money.

Around Lew there's an entirely different set of people and an entirely different emphasis. This will shake down through the company, and will be felt even by the man who sweeps out the chips in the tool room.

Now then, what has all this to do with your place and conduct in the conference?

Just this. Take a look at that management of yours. Determine for yourself what kind of management it is.

You may never have occasion to visit the executive suite, but your chances of ever being a resident of it are greatly influenced by your understanding of who runs your company and the kind of thinking that dominates the men at the top. They are very likely to be of the same mind.

If it's a banker-type management which has little interest in engineering, don't go upstairs with drawings for a sensational new model. It would be better to look for some dramatic new way to bring the company stock to the attention of the security analysts.

If your management is sales-minded, don't expect a big bonus for your idea for simplifying office procedure and therefore reducing overhead. Rather, bring in a new slogan that will dramatize the new model changes.

In conference, knowledge of your management and how it thinks will be an invaluable aid to you. If your idea, or your approach to a problem, is in tune with the management's temperament, your thinking becomes important to management and so do you.

Now perhaps you're saying, "But we've got a banker-type management like the one you've described and I'm more the Lew type." Then why not go shopping for a new management and be sure you hire one that's going to build a sound future for *you?*

There is no thought that you should submerge your character in favor of the company character. Rather . . . join one that's agreeable to you. It's the difference between swimming upstream all your life and going with the current.

11

The Empty Chair

At EVERY BUSINESS CONFERENCE, whether it is convened in the executive suite or on the production floor, there's an empty chair. It stands at the head of the table and dominates the proceedings. It speaks with a big, booming, silent voice that rings with authority. No one, not even the president or the chairman of the board, can shout it down.

The chair is occupied by a strange and unaccountable combination of exigencies, experiences, opinions and philosophies which have accumulated through the years of corporate life and have emerged as a nebulous set of beliefs that have taken on the authority of law. This accumulation has a name. It is called "Company Policy."

Like electricity, no one is quite sure where Company Policy comes from or what it is, but everyone is quite familiar with what it does. Since it is undoubtedly the most formidable influence at the conference table let's try to find a place to stand where we can get an overall view of this monster.

Anyone who attempts to examine Company Policy—any Company Policy—is in the position of the blind man feeling the elephant's tusk and judging from that what the rest of the animal looks like. Any one policy of a company is likely not to make sense when measured against a particular situation. This, however, doesn't mean that all Company Policy is nonsense.

It is, for example, a policy of the United States Steel Corporation (at this writing, at least) to prohibit its office employees from taking a morning "coffee break." There's no way short of bootlegging to get around this dictate, either by sending out for it or bringing a percolator into the office. This doesn't necessarily mean that the corporation has a grudge against Brazil or that its medical consultants are convinced that coffee is bad for the heart. Maybe it thinks coffee breaks are too expensive in lost time, or perhaps bad for morale. Whatever it means, it's policy . . . just as it's policy at Procter and Gamble to serve coffee to the office employees at 10:30 every morning.

General Electric bends over backwards to keep alive the memory of Thomas Edison, but Westinghouse never promotes the equally brilliant record of its founder. Why? Well, it's Company Policy.

It is important to the man who is trying to understand his company or advance in it, or sell to someone else's company, to accept Company Policy as a serious fact . . . a powerful ally at the conference table to the man

who will take time to understand the policy and the thinking behind it.

Policy grows like a hedge gone wild. New shoots are always springing up, dead wood accumulates and sometimes threatens to choke the life out of the plant. If you can accept this analogy in lieu of a definition perhaps we can get down to the roots in this policy matter.

First, let's take up the new shoots. These are the easily recognized dictates, pronouncements and rules of the management which are often called policy, but which could also be called Current Operating Procedures.

This branch of policy will usually change with the management. Going back to the preceding chapter for a moment, let's consider how a single policy might be handled under the banker-type management and then under the sales executive, "Lew"-type management.

You will remember how the banker-type management organized its administrative authority by setting up autonomous departments to handle engineering, sales, personnel and so on. To fortify this organization such management is likely to establish a rigid chain of command; channels of communication will be set up and strictly adhered to. This protocol will be part of the Company Policy and woe to the salesman or employee who tries to shortcut the established channels.

It takes only a little examination to see why such a policy would be established under the banker-type management. You will remember that this management came in from the outside, has very little nuts-and-bolts knowledge of the business. If the president were caught unprepared by an outside engineer, for instance, he might very well be unable to talk about the company's product with this visiting expert.

Now suppose Lew takes over the management. One of the first changes is likely to be the establishment of an open-door policy. Lew, arriving through the sales channel, believes in open communication between individuals and departments. He will have little use for formal channels. At his first meeting he's likely to make a speech that goes something like this: "This is a big company all right, but it's not so big that the management can't find time to listen to a new idea. From now on all doors are open around here."

Lew can afford to take this stand since there's not much of importance that a salesman doesn't know about the company and its product. An accountant might catch him short, to be sure, but Lew wouldn't care if he did.

Thus, policy changes with the needs of the management. Study the policy and you will learn a lot about how to sell your plans to the men behind it.

But there's another branch of the policy tree that is not so simple to cope with or to understand. It's the dead wood we spoke of earlier.

In the American business scene nothing is more worshiped than experience. Almost without exception management is fanatically devoted to it.

The worst thing you can say about a man, the very worst, is that he lacks experience. This ends all further consideration of him or what he has to say.

What this cult of experience worshipers doesn't realize is that while experience is very often a valuable asset, it can also be a drastic liability.

What has this to do with Company Policy? Well, that's where the dead wood often creeps in to choke the life out of the plant.

How many business concerns are operating today at half their potential because the management relies on its experience rather than its judgment? Now the old-timer who usually begins the "Now it's always been Company Policy . . ." will maintain that there can be no judgment without experience. Which is the same as saying that no man can do anything he hasn't done before.

The advocate of "It's always been Company Policy . . ." doesn't mean to tell a lie, but he's not speaking the truth. What he really should say is, "Back in 1932 we tried out an idea and it worked; we don't remember how or why it worked, but we still believe in it."

This idea, whatever it was, met the needs of the depression, perhaps it even saved the company. Old-timer believes in it like he believes in Heaven above. It's part of Company Policy. The fact that it fails to meet the need of the new times doesn't matter. It's still policy. And sometimes the cost of these anachronisms is appalling.

The writers have had some experience working with the automotive business. Periodically, the car manufacturers find themselves engulfed in their own product. Five or ten thousand cars must be moved off the premises today to make way for tomorrow's production. Meanwhile all the pipelines are full and dealers are screaming for mercy.

Now the auto business, more than any other, is run by men of vast experience in moving automobiles. Their antidote for these periodic emergencies is to draw on their rich and colorful past. Company Policy has always been to put on more pressure when the going gets tough. Make the dealers carry bigger inventories, insist that they add more salesmen, step up local and national advertising, encourage big local sales promotions which usually amount to price-cutting wars.

Many policy makers in the automobile business have been so engrossed in making their policy work that they haven't noticed some changes that have come over America since the Twenties when these methods were developed.

In those days there were a few principal thoroughfares where the neighborhood did its buying. This was usually on a trolley-car line, with the retailers clustered around the trolley stops. It was logical to place automobile dealerships in that location. It was logical, also, to treat the coming out of a new model as an event of national importance. The public responded to these tactics. Everyone stopped in to see the latest merchandise from Detroit, whether or not he was in a position to invest. It became routine to be informed on the new automotive triumphs, just as you were informed about the local ball club. Today's old-timers were young in the business then and they came to believe in this system like they believed in Mother.

Meanwhile, the cities spread out, throughways were built so motorists could avoid these traffic-snarled retail streets. Shopping centers began popping up at the edge of town. Rapid-transit systems and express bus service replaced the trolley cars. There was no longer a need to go into the old retail areas. Realizing this, the chain drugstores, the food stores, the sewing machine centers, the sporting goods shops, everyone who had something to sell, located their establishments in the new congregation centers. That is, everyone except the automobile people. They rode along on the post-war market, the policy makers still believing in their success of bygone years.

Dealerships went modern: acres of plate glass, glaring lights, tremendous investment. Sales and service facilities for the same make of car duplicated every few blocks. Dealers were buying yachts, sales managers were beaming, production facilities doubled, trebled, quadrupled.

And then the pipeline filled up with cars.

Mr. Car Buyer no longer sprained an ankle to see the new model. He yawned, fired up the old family bus and drove out to the shopping center to spend his money. There amid pleasant, modern surroundings he could buy everything he needed . . . except an automobile. For an automobile he had to drive down to the old trolley-car stop; that's the only place automobiles were sold.

And when he got there he could find no place to park. Behind the plate-glass windows, in the glare of lights, half a dozen hungry-looking salesmen stood waiting for him. This was a forbidding, even frightening setup. Waiting for the traffic light to change he got to thinking maybe the old bus was good for another year, and drove on.

These are wide-open fields for the alert young executive. Question particularly those policies which are so deep-seated in company organization and procedure that they seem almost beyond question.

Therein lies the greatest opportunity for spectacular improvement.

A reverse example is the case of The Hoover Company. Back in 1907 The Hoover Company was in the business of making horse collars and saddlery, had been for over a quarter of a century. But there were beginning to be a few automobiles chugging through the ruts of America, and The Hoover Company had an opportunity to make leather straps for supporting the tops of automobiles. These straps fastened to the tops above the windshield and then went forward to be anchored at the fenders.

Now it had been Company Policy not to do anything which would affront the harness makers who were the principal customers of the Hoover saddlery. Obviously automobiles were an affront to the harness makers.

However, The Hoover Company, in the manner of men making a grave decision—which they were—decided to do business with the auto makers, despite their Company Policy.

It turned out to be the saving of them. You can see where they would be today if they had stayed in the harness business.

However, they had to change Company Policy again, and drastically. How much leather do you see on a modern automobile? The Hoovers found many products to make for the automobile trade: crank boots, spring covers, spare tire straps, magneto covers, knuckle boots and several other items. But as fast as the Hoovers could find applications for leather in the automobile, the auto makers found a way to make those parts out of steel.

But the sons of W. H. Hoover had the astuteness to change the Company Policy drastically. They got out of the automobile business and began to make vacuum cleaners.

It should be part of your philosophy to question whether the way a thing is being done is the best way it can be done. Bring this attitude with you to the conference table. Keep it to yourself until you find an old dead-wood policy that needs pruning. Don't challenge it until you are well fortified with facts and statistics.

A man in Cleveland, Ohio, named Robert Heller has built a large and well-known organization on the business of changing other people's Company Policy. After studying a firm thoroughly, but with the freshness of an outsider, he may recommend that a golf club manufacturer stop making golf clubs and start making garden tools. And the information upon which he will base this violent decision has been at the disposal of the managers of the company for many years. But the Heller organization is not limited by long indoctrination to the Company Policy.

You'll be amazed, we think, at the opportunities that exist to make major improvements in Company Policy. And the older and more successful the company, the more such opportunities you are likely to find.

And remember, whether or not Company Policy is being discussed at the conference table, it is still there, sitting in that high and mighty chair, speaking with that booming, silent voice. The more you know about it the better your opportunity to bring its tremendous influence to bear on your side of the question.

Know your Company's Policy—go along with it or change it; but don't try to make it the fall guy for your own shortcomings.

12

Humor in the Conference

Have you ever tried to rub your head and pat your stomach at the same time? Humor is that way. You can't laugh and be mad at the same time, even in a conference.

In Boston there is a young man who has a fabulous reputation for making money and friends. Regarded as a financial wizard, John Fox has many projects in operation, one of them being the Boston *Post*; all of them being money makers. Among multimillionaires he is such a youngster that an observer is apt to decide that Fox must surely be a cold, shrewd, scheming man.

Actually he's a kind, sentimental Irishman who hates to hurt anyone, hates to bludgeon his opinion through a meeting or override his fellow man.

Yet obviously he didn't fill up several bank accounts by deferring to other people's judgment. And he does have an explosive temper which he controls carefully. But one day his chief financial adviser, John Faxon, opposed him consistently on a point in conference. Fox blew up in anger. It was a rolling barrage of spontaneous wrath which blasted Faxon for ten minutes straight.

Suddenly Fox noticed the room was shocked into hurt, sullen and embarrassed silence.

He came to his senses. He grinned. 'I'll have to apologize for Faxon, gentlemen. He loses his temper."

Laughter rocked the room. Good feeling and sudden affection for Fox put the meeting back on the good road.

Sam Goldwyn, the great motion picture producer, had a problem. He approached L. B. Mayer of M-G-M. "Louis," he said with straight-faced concern, "we're both in trouble."

"How come?" Mayer wanted to know.

"Well, it's about Clark Gable."

"How could you and I both be in trouble about Gable?" Mayer wanted to know with some pique and much surprise.

"You got him. I want him." Goldwyn grinned.

They sat down to make a deal.

At one point in the Army-McCarthy hearings when tempers were short, army counsel Joseph N. Welch was accused of being out to "get" Mr. Carr's job and his "neck." Carr was on McCarthy's staff. Welch said, "Sir, even if I were to succeed, I wouldn't know how to dispose of either."

Even Welch's opponents worked hard at stifling grins.

But Welch continued in his slow, mild way, "I don't hate Mr. Carr. Why at some future date I may find myself opposed to him in some court of law. I may even lose to him. And if I do, I will walk over to him afterward and congratulate him. Losing a case to Mr. Carr wouldn't upset my life. Why I have a perfect *genius* for losing cases."

The tight-faced conferees, all attorneys, burst out simultaneously in loud laughter and Mr. Welch had his way that day.

Just in passing, the wide-open invitation of Mr. Welch to laugh at himself as a great loser of cases brought with it the subtle but very firm suspicion that he had never lost a case in his life.

The joke doesn't even need to be very funny. If it gives everybody an excuse to laugh they can be agreeable without losing face. And once your opponent laughs . . . well, just try to laugh and be mad at the same time. Try it.

About the toughest conference Jack Dempsey ever faced was after the fight with Gene Tunney on the night of September 3, 1926, in Philadelphia.

Back in his hotel room was a crowd of reporters plus the host of friends who had been accustomed to join Dempsey in the victory celebration which had lately become inevitable after every fight.

He needed these friends, too, because the crowds at the ringside were not in his corner lately. Oh, while he was on the way up he was tremendously popular, of course. But after he knocked down a string of first-rate fighters including the handsome French war hero Georges Carpentier, it got to be too much. Dempsey took on the aspect of an unbeatable monster. And the roar of the crowd was for the underdog. This night the crowd was for Gene Tunney.

The news of the Tunney fight reached the hotel room long before Dempsey.

Dempsey didn't win.

The air was taut as they waited for the Manassa Mauler to come back to the hotel.

This had never happened before. What would one say to Dempsey? What would Dempsey say? How would he act?

Dempsey shoved open the door and the crowd of reporters and guests was silent. No one knew how to begin, The seconds stretched out awkwardly.

Finally Dempsey's wife, the former Estelle Taylor, asked, "What happened?"

And remember Jack's classic answer?

"Honey," he said, "I forgot to duck."

That's all he said, but it made a national hero of Jack Dempsey, the man who could toss away the crown with a joke. They respected Dempsey before. But now they loved him.

Big Bill McClusky bought out the telephone company in Rock Creek, Ohio. He was a big man for size and he was a big man for modernization. When he took over, his first move was to try to get the people to call by number instead of asking the operator, "Let me talk to Miller."

"Which one? Jack Miller?"

"No. You know I never call Jack. Fred, I want."

All this was time-consuming and McClusky printed a new phone book and urged them to use the numbers. But on this the people pretty much defeated him. And there were grumblings about the new management of the telephone company.

McClusky's countermove was to put in dial equipment. That way the people had to use the numbers, and McClusky's payroll was smaller. But McClusky was still very much the outsider in town. In his effort to win over the town he joined the volunteer fire department, and served in every way he knew. But they still took potshots at him, and every meeting of any kind was always a sales conference for Bill McClusky.

He kind of broke the ice one night at a volunteer firemen's meeting, though. After McClusky finished reciting his too complete views on what kind of improvements could be made in the fire truck, one of the men bawled out, "By the way, McClusky, how many dissatisfied telephone customers you got now?"

Bill was going to snap back a short answer. But instead he grinned. 'Let's see," he counted up mentally, "countin' you, it's exactly 416."

It was hard not to be on McClusky's side after that.

In the cantankerous steel industry, where the leaders grow big and still talk loud and rough in the great tradition of Taylor, Carnegie and Morgan, a gentler voiced man now emerges. Benjamin Franklin Fairless, out of Stark County, Ohio, is tough enough; but the problems facing the steel industry today are subtler than before.

As president of U. S. Steel, Ben Fairless often had need to cajole all the competing steel companies into presenting a solid front. For this purpose, high-level, industry-wide conferences were called, and they tended to be stormy.

In one such meeting a physically huge steel maker from the Midwest was loudly berating a stiff-jawed steel man from New England, who had his own followers at the meeting and who happened to be physically small. The split which was developing threatened to put a critical gulf in the industry at a crucial time.

Fairless said, "Please, gentlemen, even in this ring we never match a bantam against a heavyweight."

Laughter put the meeting back into Fairless's capable hands.

13

It's All in How You Say It

Maybe there's another way to put it. When you have a sound proposal, but seem to come up against a blank wall continually . . . you may be coming up against just plain words.

Words can be murder. You would think that words were precision instruments, being precisely defined in dictionaries so that grammar school students understand them. But they are not precision instruments. Whole professions exist because words are not precision instruments. Attorneys and judges and arbiters and advertising men frequently are involved in nothing but determining what a particular word means.

In the Selden-Ford patent suit 3,600 pages of testimony and six years of time were consumed over the question, What is meant by the word invention?

Nations go to war because a word is not precise. Partnerships break up because a word has two meanings to two people sitting in the same office . . . some common word, usually.

The reason for your battle of words is simple. In a conference you are not fighting the dictionary definition of a word. You are fighting the definition of a word which is in the other man's head. That is the only definition of any importance.

Here's how it can happen. When you use the word "tomorrow," you mean the twenty-four-hour period of time beginning immediately after midnight tonight and extending through the next twenty-four hours. But if, on a Monday, you were to ask a Philippine native to build you a grass hut "tomorrow," he might not begin work until Friday, because in his language "tomorrow" merely means "the future."

Now it is not much of a stretch from that situation to your conference. To some men around that table "tomorrow" means the eight hours next day between nine and five. To another it means any time next day up to midnight. To some, it even means sometime in the future. In fact, we often use the word "tomorrow" poetically or figuratively to mean "the future."

In a business conference you may have used a word which stuck in the craw of a man. He assigned to that word some meaning which you might have no way of knowing.

The sales manager of a large apparatus manufacturer was having a meeting of his distributor management. His distributors were good men, carefully chosen, successful. But they had reached the point where they felt that any increase in *volume* of their present activity was gained at too much additional cost.

Now this is a common attitude, and is true that after a point additional *volume* is gained at additional sales expense which may reduce percentage of profit. No one, the sales manager included, wanted to deny this. But his point was that additional profit, even at a smaller rate, is still desirable. And you can't stand still without slipping back.

But the distributors, he knew, had been overexposed to talk about *increased volume*. If he started with those words, their ears would be half closed before he could make his point. He decided there must be another way to put it.

He, therefore, did not mention *increased volume* as such, but he talked in this vein: "If you took the names and product signs off all American places of business, you would find we are all basically in the same business. And that business is the business of turning over dollars. We all start with dollars, and hope by turning them over often enough—via investment in a product which we sell —to come out of the transaction with a profit for ourselves on the transaction of dollars. Therefore, the more often we can turn over those dollars the more profit we make. Everything else being equal, say a man makes a good profit by turning over his dollars three times a year, then he will make more profit if he can manage to turn over his dollars four times a year."

The sales manager then proposed that each distributor attempt to turn over his dollars one more time per year. "Turning over dollars one more time" is the same as increasing volume, of course; and everyone knows it. There was no attempt to conceal the message. That is not the point. But "turning over dollars" was a new way of saying "increased volume"—which caught the attention of his distributor audience long enough so that he could get their good attention to his line of reasoning.

After his address the sales manager was told by several distributors that his plan of attack made good sense. One man said, "In fact it gets right down to the reason for being in business."

The Harris brothers, founders of Harris-Seybold, discovered that a *number* was their stumbling block. They had engineered a new printing press which would register fifteen thousand impressions an hour on a type of job where the standard had been about two thousand impressions per hour.

Elated with their new product, they went out to invite the printing industry to watch a demonstration of their new press "which will print fifteen thousand copies per hour."

The claim seemed so fantastic and the prospects were so incredulous that the Harrises received answers like this: "Look, if you can print fifteen thousand copies an hour, I would have heard about it."

Another: "Mr. Harris, I do not have time to go running around looking at any novelty so tricked up that it can print 700 per cent faster than existing presses."

The Harris brothers were dumbfounded. Their press was too good to be believed.

They decided to change their story. On their next call they said, "Sir, we'd like you to come to our plant next

Friday to watch a demonstration of our new high-speed press."

"Well, just how high speed is it?"

"Well, sir, this may sound fantastic. But it will print over five thousand impressions an hour."

With this revised advance billing the Harrises were able to turn out a good crowd to watch the press work.

Mr. W. W. Steele was sales manager of The Hoover Company, makers of vacuum cleaners in North Canton, Ohio. One of their principal methods of distribution was the famous 'Hoover Man," who comes to your door to demonstrate the cleaner.

In the early 1930's, however, a wave of anti-canvasser ordinances began to be passed by city councils across this country.

The Hoover Company watched this with some alarm. When William Steele noticed in the papers that such an ordinance was passed in Wilmette, Illinois, he decided it was time for some action. He boarded a train and went up to Wilmette.

There he found that the ordinance had been sparked by three housewives. He asked their names and went to call on them. He found that their husbands all worked for companies which existed by selling industrial products to industry. He assembled the wives to see if he could make them aware of certain unfair aspects to the anti-canvasser ordinance; and to do it, he used not his vocabulary, but theirs. Here is how he reasoned:

"The largest industry in America today is housekeeping. In this industry the purchasing agent is the housewife. Her office is the home. All we are doing is the same thing your husbands do. We go to the purchasing agent in her office."

The three wives were listening closely.

"Now you have put through a rule that keeps us from talking to the purchasing agents who buy our products. Would that not be equivalent to our passing a rule at The Hoover Company that your husbands could not come to see our purchasing agent to sell us motors?"

The three women nodded.

Steele continued, "Now we will be quite happy to have our salesmen register or whatever you like; but we think it quite unfair to separate us from our purchasing agents."

The ordinance was rescinded. It was a matter of a different way of saying it . . . which is to say, a different way of looking at it. Today the Hoover Man who calls at homes is an affectionately regarded part of American folklore.

Mark Twain said: "The difference between the right word and the almost right word is the difference between the lightning and the lightning bug."

The "right word" decisively won a showdown-type conference in an open meeting of a village of five thousand. The argument was zoning. The situation was a typical condition now occurring all over America. Men who worked in the nearby city of Cleveland were pushing way out into the suburbs to establish residence in the middle of a small farming village.

The rural atmosphere and the low taxes made it attractive to them for their home sites. But the presence of these newcomers in large numbers naturally decreased the rurality of the village and *increased* the work to be done by the taxes.

The village council, comprised of original residents, mostly farmers, struggled with this problem of village housekeeping for a suddenly larger population . . . schools, fire protection, police, water, sewers. In these deliberations the newcomer commuters took little interest. It was not their affair.

However, the solution the village officials reached was a new zoning program which would admit limited light industry to certain areas of the town, hoping thus to get major tax assistance without raising the existing rate on homes and farms.

Suddenly the newcomers became alert. "Industry here! No, sir!"

Now this book is not interested in the correctness of the arguments *for* industrial zoning or *against* it . . . only how each side handled itself.

There was an open meeting at which both sides were heard. Two hundred of the newcomers arrived, first time inside the town hall for most of them. About forty of them spoke.

They were their own worst witnesses.

These were for the most part competent downtown

businessmen, accustomed to large responsibility and to large conferences. Yet their argumentation against admitting industry got into descriptions of their new homes as "assets to the community," unintentionally but definitely inviting comparison to the older homes which were built long before the advent of the radar garage doors and the sectional picture window. Into their argument increasingly crept a condescending tone which said, in effect: "We can see how a farm wouldn't be bothered by the presence of light industry, but look at us with our fancy tulip beds and patio gardens."

But chiefly their naïve lack of understanding of the complexity, importance, science and dollar investment in farming was what showed through their conversation to set them up for a fall.

And the lightning which blasted the base of their argumentation was one word—*the* right word.

You see, as they talked, their concept of a farmer became quite clear to the whole room—a kind of muddy-booted frontiersman with a milk stool over his shoulders.

But the man who rose to speak first for the natives was a twenty-eight-year-old M.A. in a charcoal-gray suit with a white button-down collar and small-striped necktie. His face was tan and weathered; his eyes were crow-footed at the corners; his weapon was one word.

He said, "Gentlemen, we are pleased with the addition of your new houses to our community. But since you work in the city, may I explain the problems of our families who have always made our living in *agriculture*."

There was slinking down in the chairs in the small

town hall. Financial men, attorneys, manufacturing executives, engineers . . . shrunk. They had met a giant. An
agriculturist.

But the difference between a farmer and an agriculturist is only a word. And this difference is not even a
dictionary difference; it is only a difference in some men's
minds.

Industrial zoning came in.

14

How to Take Over a Job

PERHAPS THE MOST CRUCIAL CONFERENCE you will ever face will be the day you take over a new job in a new company.

Let's look around the room. You have just stepped into it. Or perhaps you were there early, and some of the others are drifting in late.

The latecomers arrive with out-thrust jaws that say, "Yes, I'm in the habit of coming late. Make something of that."

Milder men around the table watch you to see if you noticed and if you look capable of doing anything about it. Over in one corner is Old Jonesy. Fifteen years with this company. He didn't really expect to get this job that you just landed, but in point of seniority this is an awkward moment for him. But there are millions of BTU's of work in Jonesy if you can keep him on your side despite the fact that you don't really have enough gray hair in your head for this job.

Opposite you is young Wick. He studies you closely. He thought he had earned first call on the job you landed. He was just a hair too young for the job, but he's good; and he was already acting as though the job would be his, with some justification. So his position is a little awkward too. He studies you and his eyes can't quite conceal his thoughts. "Well, I'll stick for just a while and see . . ."

Then there's the real youngster around the table. Young enough to be very honest. Admiration for your predecessor is definitely registered on his out-thrust lower lip. "I doubt if you'll be half the man the Old Man was."

Seated between these perhaps are older men, more tired. "Here we go again. Another new broom."

They're men well rooted in the suburbs with family and friends and clubs. They cover the range of courage from those who'll do anything to stick to those who will cooperate within reason depending on what kind of man you turn out to be. But they're all nervous.

How shall you begin that first meeting which is so tense that they even laugh at Jonesy's old joke about the number three assembly line? Well, you've got to be yourself. But here's your number one rule: do not preoccupy yourself with your own dramatic position. Situate yourself instead in their position. Try to feel as they feel. And stress the parts of your proposed program or method of operation which is of most concern to them.

That's easy to say. But what are the actual words?

Well, you must choose them to fit your own character. But we can tell you what some others have said in that electric moment.

When Alfred E. Perlman took over the presidency of the New York Central Railroad after Robert Young's flamboyant proxy victory, Young was known as a man who made big changes, sharp and drastic. Naturally the one hundred thousand New York Central employees would expect that any president hired by Robert Young would come in with big personnel changes, and they would worry.

But Perlman announced, "I have not even brought with me my own private secretary. My first move will be to spend six months getting acquainted with the people and problems of this railroad."

Well, a man like that would seem to be a fair man. And good men don't worry when a fair man takes the helm.

The Hoover Company, makers of vacuum cleaners in North Canton, Ohio, came to a turning point where they wanted to triple production of vacuum cleaners. For this purpose Frank Hoover sought a man accustomed to operating a big mass production plant. A man of great strength, knowhow and mass production understanding.

He found Bill Bailey, a Bethlehem Steel mass production executive accustomed to handling big problems.

F. G. Hoover took Bailey in to meet the foremen.

Almost to a man they had grown up with The Hoover Company since the days when it produced only fifteen and twenty cleaners a day. They were worried.

Over the years they had each carved a certain niche for themselves. They knew where they stood. How would it be now? They studied the big outsider closely.

Bailey shook hands all around the room and then he said, "Gentlemen, I am the last man to be hired from the outside."

The room exhaled and prepared to go to work.

Ben Fairless, of U. S. Steel, stepped into this situation often in his rise. But on at least one occasion he took over with a joke on himself. That's the best kind of joke, by the way.

Early in his career Ben Fairless had just barely passed thirty years of age when he was made general manager of Central Steel. Central Steel took over another plant and Fairless' job was to step in and start running the merged company. That's always a ticklish moment. The executives of the absorbed firm are always nervous, suspicious, inclined to drag their feet. The atmosphere is tense.

Fairless stepped into the conference with a grin. "No management in this plant has ever lasted more than twenty-two months," he said. "We've got a lot of work to do in twenty-two months."

They were on Ben's side.

15

"How to Lose One"

THERE COMES A TIME when a man should yield a point. But don't just throw it away. There is a strategy to giving in.

The young and earnest president of a diesel locomotive manufacturing company was faced with union demands for a twelve cent per hour increase.

He was an enlightened professional manager of the new school; and if the wage increase could be justified he wished to grant it.

A four-hour session with his auditors and a thirty-minute meeting of the board of directors convinced him the raise was logical.

He called the union officials for a meeting at one o'clock the following Monday.

"You will be glad to hear," he said, "that we can meet your request for a twelve cent per hour increase."

There seemed to be no overt joy among the union officials, and the president leaned back and smiled broadly. "In fact, gentlemen, we can do better than that. There will be a fifteen cent per hour increase across the board effective April first. It will be announced on Wednesday."

On Tuesday morning at eleven o'clock the young locomotive president walked into the office of a leading firm of specialist labor law attorneys . . . bewildered, deeply hurt.

After explaining his negotiations and his generous offer he wrinkled his forehead and pounded the desk. "Will you tell me why in the world . . . of all times . . . my men struck at 9:00 this morning?"

"Of course they would," said the attorney calmly.

"Why? Why!"

"Put it this way," the attorney explained patiently. "Suppose you offered me $100,000 for my house on Bunce Road. Suppose then, without a yes or no, I shoved out my hand and said, 'Shake! It's a deal!' What would you think then?"

The diesel president fingered his chin. "Why, I guess I'd figure I'd been taken."

"Exactly," said the attorney. "That's just how your men feel."

Mr. Diesel Locomotive was suddenly a wiser man.

"Besides leaving the men with the feeling they should have asked for more, you make the union leaders look bad," continued the attorney. "You gave them the money, but you took away from them the prestige of winning a victory . . . which is sometimes more important."

When you have occasion to yield a contested point,

make them win it. They will like you for it—as men have always "liked the man who makes them like themselves a little better."

In addition, by yielding hard, allowing the man his victory, you entitle yourself to a victory in the future.

In certain situations opposition is a man's justification for existence—as in the case of the union leaders at diesel. Rob him of a fight at twelve cents, he has no alternative but to carry the business to higher ground where you *will* fight—say twenty cents. The same is true of many occupations where the function has an "agent" flavor.

On the other hand there are times when you shouldn't make them fight for it. Sometimes the reverse is more effective. One of the most successful advertising managers in this country follows a practice which gains him great acceptance and respect. I watched him in an arduous two-hour session one day in which he battled for forty minutes for a particular advertising program. When he finally yielded the floor the opposite-minded men attacked his plan in loud voices one after another, right around the table. When the last man had spoken the air was thick with cigar smoke and a little fire. Temples were red and tempers were short. The men were braced for an aggressive rebuttal.

But the advertising manager leaned back, closed his eyes as if thinking a moment. Then he rocked forward and grinned. "Gentlemen, you're right. I withdraw my idea."

It took a second for the room to grasp what he

had done, but the relaxation and admiration were almost audible as the men around the table exhaled and unwound.

The men adjourned for lunch and you could hear fragments of conversation. "Takes a big man to concede flat out like that." . . . "Now if it had been Shaw we'd still be—" . . . "Like to work with a guy like that."

Just as only a rich man can afford to wear a baggy old suit, it would seem to be true that it takes a big man to give in. It may have been pure coincidence, but I happened to observe that when we reconvened for the afternoon session, the advertising manager's whole program went through the approval mill without a hitch or an objection. In fact it seemed to me men were eager to find good points about it.

Above all when it comes to yielding, if you are persuaded that you have been in error, give in. It *is* possible to bludgeon through an idea or a policy in which you have lost conviction, but if you succeed you are worse off. If it is a matter of any importance, and if you prove to be wrong, the policy will come back to haunt you many times. If it proves to be a mistake, your opponents will love to put your name on it; and even a strong man defending a mistake after he knows it's a mistake, is a Samson with a crew cut. It often follows that to defend this mistake you must defend other parallel mistakes in order to be consistent. Your words lose weight in future conferences.

16

Hire the President

PUT THE PRESIDENT and top brass to work for you. Fred Buford talked to us one day for the special purpose of letting us in on his big dream. He is a smart man with a brain that is always whirling. He works for a large sales consulting organization and over the years he had worked out an integrated plan for selling which he believed to be a winner. It was quite different, and it had the great power of simplicity and genuine service to the customer.

He told us about it because he wanted us to execute one part of it which fell within our field. To sell his idea at the high level it required, he needed to assemble a sample of his program.

He had worked out the idea in such detail and had researched it at such expense and labor that he was sure of its workability. As we listened to the proposal, we were sure he had a winner, even discounting twenty per cent for the enthusiasm which glittered in Fred's eyes.

After the explanation, he lowered his voice some. "Now, I ask you to keep this confidential. I'm basing my whole future on it."

"What do you mean, Fred?"

"Well, it's quite different from the kind of thing my firm does. I'll have to resign and take it to a different company. I have three in mind that will be naturals for it, and I've got to find a way to get to Mr. Johanson at General Motors. If he sees this, he'll want it."

"Fred, is your company paying you enough money?"

He looked startled. "I get a good salary!"

"Do you like the outfit?"

"Sure do. I'll hate to leave. Why?"

"Well, Fred, this idea of yours is a big one. You realize you've got to get top-level attention for it, don't you?"

"Yes, and that's a problem. I don't know anyone at Avco or General Motors."

"But Mr. Byrd, the president of your own company, has been operating in those circles for years, and your company has a big name."

"Oh, sure." Fred expanded with some pride. "Jim Byrd walks into the fourteenth floor of the GM building once a month. Knows 'em all up there by their first names."

"And he knows five or six top people at ALCOA, and a half dozen at Union Carbide and at General Electric. In fact, there's hardly a major concern in this country where your boss can't call up and be welcome, is there, Fred?"

"Huh. Guess that's right."

"Those he doesn't know in person probably know about him, don't they, Fred?"

"That's right."

"So the best man on the face of the earth to promote your idea is your *own* boss, Jim Byrd."

"No," Fred said emphatically. "Our company doesn't handle things like this. Besides, I'm . . . you know, I've been there five years. I'm just home folks there. The idea wouldn't get the right kind of really serious attention."

There are thousands of Fred Bufords in this country, bright men, hard working, ambitious. They spend five, ten, fifteen years with a company; then they get the idea of a lifetime.

Immediately they think it's a natural for the ABC Company or the XYZ Company. They can quickly think of three firms who have the stature and the size to make the best employment of their idea.

The last place they consider is their own company.

In his search for people who can help him market or develop his idea, Fred Buford seeks the most powerful alliances he can make. But he doesn't consider the very people with whom he has spent the past ten years building confidence and trust and a credit balance of favors. He blithely throws away his strongest ally.

Somehow he thinks that in a half hour with the president of General Motors he could sell his idea better than in ten years with his own firm.

Now there is good reason for this. We are not deriding. Vaguely Fred senses that his own management will not be sympathetic to his biggest-idea-in-a-lifetime. And he may be right. What he is combatting is the "home folks" familiarity which makes it hard to see the brilliance of a fellow who's "been around here for five years."

But the beauty of this is that it can be licked. You see this is a two-way street. It's true that Jim Byrd is guilty of thinking of Fred as "just home folks." But Fred is also guilty of considering Jim Byrd "just home folks." So when he presents his ideas to Byrd—that's a conference—he makes a casual, "old shoe," offhand, incomplete presentation. He gives Byrd none of the benefit of his best salesmanship, leaving it up to Byrd to fill in details and sell himself on it. He selects a setting where he does his routine business with Byrd, at a routine time, in a routine tone of voice. Byrd thinks it's a routine idea.

We said, "Fred, you could look for five years and never find a man who is in a position to push this idea, for you like Jim Byrd. That is, one who knows you well enough to give you a fair hearing."

"That's just the trouble, he knows me *too* well."

"Right. But suppose you go back to your company, make an appointment with Byrd just as though you were an outsider, through channels if necessary."

"What! Make an appointment with my own boss?"

"Yes. And tell him you did it that way because you want him to think of you as an outsider and look only at your idea. Tell him you considered going elsewhere just because of that familiarity. Then present the program as elaborately as you would to a stranger. Tell him you want him to grab this ball and run with it, and tell him you want him to take it to GM, and you want to go with him."

Fred leaned back and grinned. "Well, I'll be darned!"

Fred had a little trouble about the appointment business. That is, there were a couple layers of vice presidents between Fred and his boss. But he took them along with him, asking them to join him in this project which he billed as a new business venture.

There was a lot of eyebrow raising about this formal appointment rigmarole. And Fred lifted them even farther by hiring a hotel room for the meeting. He said it was to prevent interruptions, but really it was to change the setting. The men arrived with quizzical expressions and Byrd said, "What in hell is going on around here?"

Best thing that could have happened.

Fred presented his integrated sales program. It was a big hit.

Now it would be better for us if we could report that Jim Byrd immediately grabbed the idea and rushed it to the president of General Motors. He didn't. He selected three other companies which he thought would be more natural for it. Since the program requires major changes in a conventional sales organization, it is not sold at the present writing. But from our point of view, it is an overwhelming success.

Here's why.

Beginning at three o'clock on the Monday afternoon on which that first meeting was held in the hotel room, Jim Byrd took a new look at Fred Buford. Maybe he didn't pay as much attention to the idea as he did to

Fred Buford. Presidents are dumb that way. So dumb was Jim Byrd that he set up a special department with the exclusive assignment of continually developing new programs like Fred's.

So dumb was Jim Byrd that he put Fred Buford in charge of this department and gave him a raise.

Put to work for yourself all the resources and people of your company. You're entitled to them. You are turning over to the company your ability and your good name.

You probably know of ten men outside your company who would like to get to see the head of your department to enlist his support for a project. Ten men who would give plenty to have his ear under favorable circumstances for a half hour. You have him right handy five days a week, fifty weeks a year.

Hire him.

Now you may well reply—with truth—"But I did give my company a superior idea just last August. And nothing happened about it."

If your good ideas have a habit of getting lost in the firm—well, that's why this book was prepared. You lost a conference. Never thought of it as a conference, did you? It was. And every conference—that's every single one—is a contest. Something is sold or not sold.

"But if a good idea is such a natural for the company —my own company at that—why should it *have* to be sold?"

Let's not go into that. Everything has to be sold. And often the better it is, the harder the selling.

Twenty years before the Wintons and Fords and
Duryeas came along, George B. Selden had the patent
on the automobile. Couldn't sell it to a soul. John Fitch
went broke trying to sell somebody a steamboat. The
very best thing in the world is "peace on earth and good
will toward men." But in twenty centuries we haven't
built any salesmen good enough to sell that. Are your
ideas better than those?

If you get a good hearing for your idea and then
nothing happens, don't quit. Perhaps your timing was
off. Bring it out again when some crisis in the company
makes it suddenly more vital and important. If the idea
was really good there will come a juxtaposition of circumstances which make it suddenly obvious.

Insurance men who spend several years on a rugged
prospect who derides the whole subject of insurance
are often surprised to get a phone call out of the blue.
Suddenly the man sees the point of insurance very
clearly. He wants to sign up right *now*. When they get to
his house they see why. He's sick.

When your company is sick in one of its departments,
suddenly your pigeonholed idea can become good med-
icine. But you have to watch for the symptoms and
write out your prescription all over again. When there's
trouble, it's easiest to win the conference. So how long
is it since you've repeated your suggestion?

Or maybe you have had a lot of them. Make a list of
them, and decide that each one is going to be a major
project that will require as much hammering as it took
to sell the automobile. When you get one checked off

as "in effect," it becomes easier to push the next one over the hump. But keep books on them, and follow up.

Another mistake you may have made: in presenting your idea perhaps you left no piece of it for anyone else to put his name on. Don't just throw your idea out on the table for everyone to assess at will until you have examined it to find the advantages in it for the other men around that table. When you have found these advantages, don't trust the men to see their own personal benefit in it. Spell it out for them and give them a place to credit themselves with it.

Perhaps your byline was splashed across it too big. If your idea becomes too obviously labeled as "that Fredrickson idea" or "the Fredrickson plan," it engenders the very definite, subconscious reaction, "All right, it's Fredrickson's ball. Let Fredrickson carry it!" If you want some line-backing or some blocking, keep your eye off that grandstand.

The Big Contact

Even Tony Frascatti fell victim to the great myth of our day—the big contact. It's no wonder he did in an age when children are sent away to prep school in hopes they will make "the big contact," in a day when parents brazenly instruct their career-bent children to be alert for "contacts," in a business society which has created a whole profession baldly labeled "contact men."

This is not to say that the philosophy of the big contact is unsound. It's extremely sound and very important, almost necessary. The trouble is that most of us, like

Tony Frascatti, don't know where to look for it. Tony found out, though.

Frascatti was a carpenter, a good one. He had in mind to start his own contracting business when the time was right. But he wanted that big contact first. He found it, once removed, in the person of a young plumber with whom he had worked. If Frascatti would set up the new construction corporation on paper and put up some money and hire some men, the plumber would go to New York City where "the big contact" would arrange for the brand-new corporation to land the contract to build five good-sized buildings out in Ohio. The plumber's word had been good before. Tony had reason for confidence.

The plumber went off to New York to contact the contact. Tony went to work with some nervousness but with great hopes of setting up the corporation. He paid $250 to get the charter and the seal and a big corporation book. He arranged to hire two more carpenters and he talked to suppliers who guaranteed him good delivery on lumber, cement block, structural steel. Tony checked on a few other details and then he went down to the train to meet the plumber who was returning with the good word from the big contact.

"The word is not yet, Tony," said the plumber. "Be a couple more weeks yet."

This made Mrs. Frascatti nervous but Tony told her, "Big men like this one in New York don't move fast. But when they do, they move big. It will be all right."

But in another week the plumber seemed to have lost

faith in his big contact. He went out to look for work.

Tony Frascatti couldn't drop the new corporation so lightly as his partner. He had a lot of money in it. Also a lot of reputation. He couldn't go to work for another contractor when all his fellow carpenters knew he was in business for himself. They had even had a big party for him.

Mrs. Frascatti told Tony to go out and find some small jobs. But Tony was in so deep he needed a *big* job. Also, for small jobs you don't set up a fancy corporation complete with legal papers. Tony said he would personally go to New York and see "the big contact." Mrs. Frascatti didn't think they could afford the money for the railroad fare. But Tony went. Mrs. Frascatti packed a lunch to save one meal on the diner. Four days later she went down to the station to meet the train.

When Tony got into the car he didn't say anything about the big contact; and Mrs. Frascatti didn't need to ask.

The next morning Tony told her not to say anything to anybody anymore about the new construction corporation. He took a lunch and went out to a big construction job to sign on as a carpenter. But that's when Mrs. Frascatti took over.

She deliberately went next door to borrow a cup of coffee, of which she had plenty. She explained about Tony's new corporation. The neighbor on the south was interested.

Next Mrs. Frascatti went to the neighbor on the north

side to borrow a lemon. She told the north neighbor
that Tony's new corporation could use some business.

When Tony came home that night Mrs. Frascatti said
that the north neighbor wanted him to build a sun porch.

"One sun porch does not amount to much," Tony said.

But he built the sun porch and Mrs. Frascatti pointed
it out to the mailman whom she invited in for a cup of
coffee.

"Tony has his own construction company now, you
know," she explained to the mailman. "Business is a little
slow right now, though."

The mailman said, "Is that so?" And he left.

But when he came back the next day he said, "Mrs.
Heiler two streets over is looking for someone to finish
off her second floor. I told her about Mr. Frascatti. She
wondered if he'd stop over tonight."

Tony started work on Mrs. Heiler's upstairs, and Mrs.
Frascatti told her butcher—where she'd traded six years
—about Tony's construction business. The butcher was
very interested. He laughed and said now Tony would
have some problems that independent butchers had had
for years. But he also said, "My bacon and ham man is
going to build a new shed for his new trucks. I'll tell him
about Tony."

Mrs. Frascatti also told the grocer and the milkman and
a couple of Tony's old bosses.

But before she had even told them about it, Tony's
next-door neighbor had told all his other neighbors.
It was amazing to Tony how many of his neighbors had

garages to build and breezeways to close in and second floors to finish.

"Why didn't you tell us, Tony?" they asked.

Tony hired back the two men he had hired when he started the company.

It was more amazing to Tony how his plain old neighbors and friends had other friends and relatives who bought contracting for larger and larger companies.

Tony never did hear from the big contact in New York City, but he found a bigger one. Because when your everyday friends and neighbors and the fellow at the next desk take over your cause, they put into action a network of contacts that will reach any place you want —to contractors, publishers, architects, generals, governors, admirals, senators, butchers, bakers, and candlestick makers. Or if they don't they have aunts and uncles who do.

Do you need a big contact? Don't look five hundred miles away. Don't even look across the street. Look in the next office. Look to the man who rides to work with you every day. Collectively he knows everybody. Tell him where you want to go. He'll get you there. He is THE BIG CONTACT.

Tony Frascatti now has four men and a truck and a backlog of orders.

17

Timing

ANY MAN who has ever driven a car, caught a fish, swung at a golf ball, closed a sale, or operated in the moonlight with a girl, knows the importance of timing.

It is even more important in the conference.

Buckholtz's idea may have no more value than last week's newspaper, but if he springs it at the right time it can carry the day. Conversely, the best idea at the wrong time won't even get off the ground.

A conference we attended recently was called in the offices of an oil company for the dead serious purpose of coming to a decision on how the company would manage to land a big turnpike contract. Only one brand of gasoline would be sold on the pike and the company had long felt that as a matter of public prestige it had to have the business regardless of the cost.

The brass was assembled, and it was fourteen-karat brass, for this was one of the most important decisions the company had faced in years. The chairman reviewed the problem. Whoever bid low enough to get the business immediately had to lay out tremendous capital to build stations every so many miles. But the bidding was so competitive, it was questionable that the investment would ever pay off.

Discussion revolved around methods of reducing the capital investment by persuading the turnpike authorities that half the number of stipulated stations would be adequate to serve the motoring needs.

Someone presented an elaborate set of statistics tending to prove that the anticipated increased sales volume would produce no additional profits unless new sources of crude oil could be found.

The conversation went on until the room was blue with smoke and heavy with gloom. The dilemma was evident but there seemed to be no solution.

Then from the back of the room a voice popped up. It had not been heard at all during the tedious deliberations, mainly because the speaker considered himself over his depth in such high level company. He was an assistant in the marketing department who had been invited only because he had helped put together one of the presentations and his department head wasn't too sure of the arrangement of facts.

The voice said, "I hope I haven't missed the main point, but there's something I don't quite understand. Why do we want to go on this turnpike anyway? Couldn't we build stations on the access roads where we wouldn't have to get into this bidding? Couldn't we send cars onto the pike with full tanks and catch 'em coming off with empty tanks? That way the stations could draw business from the nearby towns and still get a pretty good piece of the turnpike volume. Wouldn't we be better off to let someone else take the turnpike headache?"

The speech was perfectly timed.

Half an hour earlier such a suggestion would have been beneath notice; at that precise moment it was as welcome as summer rain. The suggestion, as a matter of fact, was not adopted, but it threw a whole new light on the subject and showed the way to solution. Today the assistant whose sense of timing was so unerring is high in the counsels of his company and on his way to a brilliant career.

We were present on another occasion where a conference had been called, again by the most responsible officials in a certain company to decide whether the contract for an expensive television program should be renewed. The program had been very successful, had attracted a large audience, had stimulated sales sufficient to warrant its renewal. Everyone considered it a foregone conclusion that the new contract would be signed.

The television sales people had prepared an exhaustive presentation of the program's audience ratings, its impact on the public, reflections of the good will it had built for the sponsor. It was a detailed study.

The president of the company brought the meeting to order. He asked, "How much did this program cost us last year?"

His advertising manager gave him the answer.

The president's second question was, "How did our

sales compare this year with last (before the program was on the air)?"

The sales manager answered that.

The president asked, "Then I guess we're all in agreement that it has been a good thing?"

There were affirmative nods all around.

"Very well then," the president said, "I guess there's no doubt of renewal. . . ."

At this point the television salespeople saw their wonderful presentation going for naught. The principal of this group suggested that while there was no doubt of renewal, "perhaps it might be well to take a look at the surveys that had been made. They prove beyond all doubt," he went on, "that the program is one of the most successful vehicles of the current season."

Whereupon he launched into his presentation, turning the pages lovingly, savoring the statistics. When it was over, he turned to the president, beaming with a sense of accomplishment.

The president was frowning. "I've been thinking," he said, "about the remark you made just before you launched into your talk. You said our program was the most successful of the *current* season. How do we know it will be such a hit *next* season? Maybe we've been riding the crest of a wave. I think we'd better all take another look at this thing."

"Another look" began.

It would be a better example of bad timing if we could report that the company failed to renew its contract. Actually, it did renew, but not until after several sleepless nights had passed for the salesman who failed to appreciate the importance of timing in the conference.

If hard and fast rules could be laid down for proper timing this world would be full of chiefs and there would be no Indians. For the fact is, timing is a matter of intelligence, experience, and daring. There are clues to successful timing, but no rules.

The first clue is in the atmosphere that prevails in the room at any given time. Conferences are creatures of mood. They rise to heights of optimism, plunge to depths of gloom. When an idea or suggestion for action is riding along a merry course that's no time to inject a doubt. If it's dragging along in tedious frustration, that's the time to change its course with a bright new tack.

Being forewarned of the considerations that will come up in the conference gives you time to consider the problem and perhaps to arrive at an idea for its solution. Should you burst into the room brimming with enthusiasm for your idea and get the floor immediately? Perhaps.

Or should you wait until you've heard other solutions, saving yours for the appropriate moment? Again, perhaps.

The course that might be best one day might be worst the next day. It all depends on the circumstances of the moment. Learn to sense it.

You learn this by experience. And you can learn it quickly. For example, have you had this experience?

In the middle of a routine morning you have an impulse to go across town or across the hall to talk to Ed

McGrath about a new way of packaging your company's merchandise for interstate shipment. The idea is strong in your mind right now. You put on your hat.

But as you pass your desk you see the Klamath report still unfinished, and today is the day you've allotted for that job. So you take off your hat. You go back to work on the Klamath report, merely noting on your calendar, "Call Ed McGrath *tomorrow!*"

Tomorrow comes. You go to see McGrath. But it just isn't right. You have lost the drive of yesterday, the enthusiasm. The meeting just doesn't spark. The idea dies.

There is a timing in business meetings which is important. We're apt to overmethodize ourselves. Conscientious men especially are apt to oversystemize with calendars full of appointments and schedules and target dates and phase lines. We fall in love with the idea of making these charts work out so that they become our masters. We're so interested in checking off the schedule that we can lose mobility, and the impulse opportunity is squeezed out.

Don't be afraid to cancel a meeting once in a while if something more interesting comes up which is best handled now. Too much method can kill your timing.

The important thing in timing is to remember that the conference is made up of people and people are notoriously susceptible to little things—more so in conference than in private, because moods are frighteningly contagious.

If you have faith in an idea and have failed to put it

over, don't lose your faith. There's a good chance that the time hasn't yet arrived for that idea. If it's good, if it fills a need, its time will come. There may be nothing you can do now to help it along, but the natural course of events will usually provide the opportunity.

One of the most valuable files you will ever maintain is those ideas that never saw the light. Take them to the conference with you, not on paper but in your mind. Sometime, in some conference somewhere, the time for one of them will be just right.

The best way to recognize when that time comes is to develop a healthy respect for all matters of timing. Observe old Jonesy. Chances are you will find his timing is never quite right. That's why he's just Jonesy. Observe, too, the sparkplugs of the organization—the men who have earned the respect of the others. You will find their sense of timing is unerring. They always seem to come up with the right thing at the right time.

For the quickest proof of the importance of timing, just examine the conversation of your friends. How many times, from how many people, have you heard the remark: "Why I had that idea two months ago. And I worked it all out for them down to the last detail!"

Certainly he did. The difference is timing.

18

Don't Be a Stranger

On the occasion of the firm's one hundredth anniversary, Dun and Bradstreet issued a little memory book reviewing the highlights of its history. Back in 1853, Ben Douglass, one of the founding fathers, issued a memo to the "reporters" in the field. It seems that these fellows were insufficiently zealous in their pursuit of knowledge. Mr. Douglass' memorandum read as follows:

"In some instances, it will be seen by you that our records are not so much at fault in making misstatements, as being deficient in many points that are essential to our subscribers. Where so important interests are concerned, it is necessary that they should have something definite and positive whenever it can be obtained. Is he honest? is he capable? is he responsible? should be answered in every instance, to make the report of much value. Some of our merchants regard character and capacity as of the greatest importance, while others will not sell even to an honest, capable man unless he has *capital,* particularly if he is advanced in years. Neither is it enough to say that a trader has means. An estimate of his means should be made in every case, so far as it is possible to do so. The report 'good' signifies nothing, unless we know how much the trader is good for; for as a capital of $1,000 may entitle to a certain credit, $5,000 to another and $10,000 to another, all very different in nature and extent, it is essential that we should know also, whether the applicant who is pronounced 'good' is worth $1,000, $5,000 or $10,000, or if he has no means, what makes him 'good.'

"There are many other important things to be said of every trader, such as the length of time he has been in business, in what his means consist, whether real or personal estate, or both, and whether they have been inherited or acquired, and whether the business is large or small, prosperous or otherwise, etc., etc. All these, and many others, will suggest themselves to you, but should you not be able to communicate all now, we beg you will not omit the essential facts above referred to, viz.: *character, capacity and means.*"

It is probably a safe assumption that from those days to these, D & B men have not contended themselves with merely establishing the fact that a man is "good," since this is of no value in the business world. It must also be known what a man is good *for.* Dun and Bradstreet, bless their hearts, can tell you this about anybody; which is, under the circumstances, about the most valuable service that can be imagined.

You see, we live in a world of strangers. In fact, a

man's stature in the business world can be measured in terms of the number and quality of places where he isn't a stranger. Projecting this a little further, it's even safe to say that getting ahead in the business world is simply a process of widening the circles within which you are not a stranger.

Dun and Bradstreet may rate you OK up to $25,000, which is to say, you're a stranger and not to be trusted in the $40,000 bracket. Now while Dun and Bradstreet may not be watching you, the powers-that-be in your company probably are. They too have reporters on the job and there's a file on you someplace, even if it exists only in the minds of your associates. Maybe the man who can put you into the $30,000 bracket knows you only as a $20,000 man. In other words, you're a stranger to him in any role except the one you now play. If you're going to get ahead you'll have to get acquainted with him on this new level.

The point is, that while you live with and work among a great many people who know your name, have met your wife and generally have some idea of the kind of person you are, you shouldn't conclude from this that you're no longer a stranger. To the echelon just above you're more of a stranger than if you had just walked in off the street. They are used to your presence, but not in their circle. However, there will be more resistance to admitting you to it than there would be to a total stranger.

How many times has it happened within your knowledge that someone left the company to go with another firm at a higher salary and on a higher level of responsibility? If the other outfit could recognize a good man when it saw one, why wasn't he appreciated where he was? Obviously, he was more of a stranger among his old acquaintances than he was in an entirely new group.

All too often people in business fall into the habit of cultivating strangerism. That is, within the same office they develop a narrow circle of associates to which strangers are not admitted. The same instinct is outlawed in high schools, for example, where fraternities are seldom permitted. But in the office, where there is no rule against it, this same schoolboy urge to belong to something, from which others are excluded, thrives and flourishes. If you would get ahead, confine these instincts to your membership in the Elks or the Knights of the Mystic Sea; that's what they're for. The office is a place to work, a place to expand in skill and service, and you can't do that efficiently by shutting out the strangers who come along.

Probably several salesmen call at your place of business every day. Are there people in your company who make a habit of meeting these salesmen in the lobby? If so, mark them well. They have gone about as far as they're likely to go. The visiting salesman is the most valuable stranger who ever happens by. He brings with him the latest word on the new processes and products; he knows what the competitors are doing; he probably knows what your company ought to be doing. He's a fountainhead of knowledge and a powerful, powerful enemy. He has a tough job. He has to make friends out of strangers in a

matter of seconds; he can do it, too, if he's a good salesman. Meeting him in the lobby where he's at a terrible
disadvantage will no doubt accomplish its purpose,
which is to keep him from ever getting to be anything but
a stranger to the man he's calling on. That makes two
strangers; the salesman can go on to the next call, the
man in the lobby can only go back to his office.

Just in passing, a word to the salesmen in our audience.
Your job, as stated above, is a matter of making friends,
or at least acquaintances, out of strangers in a hurry.
There's more to your job, of course, but unless you can
do that, you'll have no chance to do anything else. If
you're in the habit of counting that day lost which produced no order, or no tangible progress toward one,
figure it this way: if you have become less of a stranger
to any of your prospects, you have made considerable
progress. Even that guy who had the nerve to interview you in the lobby, if you have the grace to call on
him again, probably won't have nerve enough to do it to
you twice. This, too, is progress.

There's another phenomenon of business organization
that leaves the door of opportunity wide open to men
and women alert enough to observe it. Most business
organizations encourage internal strangerism. It becomes,
in fact, an integral part of the organization.

Architecture has something to do with it. The only
thing the people on the seventeenth floor have in common with the people on the eighteenth is the elevator.
This architectural segregation makes it convenient to
segregate departments so that accounting, for example,

can be confined to the seventeenth floor, while sales will be grouped on the eighteenth. This is a fertile situation, indeed, for the growth and culture of strangers within the company, particularly if the salesmen's expense accounts have to clear through accounting. On the seventeenth floor itself there will be divisions, architectural as well as emotional, between accounts receivable and accounts payable; just as on the eighteenth there is no friendship lost between sales and advertising.

Meanwhile this whole division with its strangers among strangers will take a dim view of, and be dimly viewed by, the people of the central division, both of whom resent and are resented by the home office people.

Where's the opportunity?

Well, the management is well aware that this divisioning and departmentalizing of the business is not good, but necessary. It realizes, more or less (with more or less alert management), that better communication between departments and divisions would result in great efficiencies all around. Somebody is always working on this problem, but nobody is ever going to solve it in a big way.

The opportunity lies with the individual who is diligent enough to establish his own communication system taking the trouble to cease to be a stranger to people in other departments.

We saw this work one time in the plant of a large manufacturer of electric motors.

Because of a situation that had developed within the electrical industry every manufacturer scrapped his old models and brought out a new line. Company A, which we were observing, had developed its pilot models and was tooling up to go into production. Meanwhile Company B, the big competitor, had moved faster and its new models were just hitting the market. Company A got its hands on one of the first Company B models to come off the line. The new motor was dissected, tested, compared in every detail. It was a good motor, but there was nothing in the design to worry Company A. Its product was just as good and in some respects a little better.

There was just one thing that worried the sales department of Company A. It had to do with the insulating material of Company B's new motor. When you took the ends off the motor to examine the windings you didn't see any wires at all. They were covered with a brick-red insulating substance that had a solid, permanent, secure look about it.

Now in selling electric motors one of the important considerations is the insulating material, for it determines the life and therefore the service you'll get from the motor.

The Company A people weren't happy about that substantial appearance of the insulation used in the B motor. In fact they were downright unhappy about it because their insulation, while superior in every respect, was a clear, transparent, plastic material. When you took the ends off their new motor to examine the windings, you could see through the insulation right through to the wires. Comparing motor A with motor B most any purchasing agent, impressed by appearances, would be likely to select the substantial red-colored insulation over the clear, transparent stuff.

The sales department of Company A expressed this worry to its development people. They ran several tests and sent back the word that the pretty red insulation of the B motor was no match for the clear homemade product because the pigments used to create the color would eventually oxidize and shorten the life of the motor. For that reason there would be no change from the clear insulation that had been planned.

The sales department people sputtered and fumed among themselves but could do nothing with the stubborn strangers in the development department.

The sales people did the only thing they could do. They called in their advertising department and explained that all sales promotion material should bear down on the advantages of clear, pigment-free insulating material.

At this point our friend Sam, a copywriter in the advertising department, entered the picture. It was his job to sell this insulation thing to the customers. Sam knew a losing proposition when he saw one. His counterpart over at Company B was no doubt pulling every stop to dramatize the advantages to the purchaser of this substantial-looking red insulating material. Probably he was arranging comparative color photographs of the two motors, with instructions to the photographer to exaggerate the transparent quality of Company A's insulation.

Sam explained to the sales department that he knew

of no advertising hocus-pocus that would overcome the disadvantages. The sales department people explained that they were well aware of the disadvantages but development had refused to budge. He'd have to do the best he could.

Well, ordinarily that would have been the end of it. Sam would have gone back to his desk to do what he could. It happened though that Sam, on previous assignments, had made it a point to go to the source of whatever it was he was writing about. For this reason he was no stranger in the development department. He called a couple of the boys.

Sam's development friends explained to him about the pigments shortening the life of the motor. Sam knew all about that. But wasn't there something they could mix with the clear plastic to make it opaque? No, there wasn't. Well, then, why couldn't they use the clear stuff as planned, but just before they put the motor together couldn't they spray something on the surface of the windings that would give them color? If the insulation was as good as they claimed, that shouldn't hurt anything.

No, it probably wouldn't hurt anything and they'd thought of that. But the production people had told them it was too late to add such a step to the line. It would mean spraying or dipping and another baking process, all of which involved considerable capital investment and more delay in getting out the new model.

Sam might have accepted that answer, but he also had friends in the production department. He looked them up. They verified everything the development people had said. But Sam felt they didn't fully appreciate the spot this put the sales department in. Would they have lunch with the sales manager? Maybe if they heard his story they might decide that the extra investment would be well worthwhile.

Sam arranged the meeting. The sales manager was, of course, very persuasive. The production people would look into it.

Well, production found a shortcut. Development found a suitable substance that would color the windings. Sales got clearance from top management. When Company A's new motors came out they had the same substantial appearance as Company B's and they've been fighting it out on that line ever since.

Incidentally, the sales manager requisitioned Sam who is now the assistant sales manager.

And that's the end of the story.

Remember, in any business situation it's natural to live within your circle of friends and exclude all strangers. It's natural to remain behind the departmental barriers and to depend upon them for your security within the company. If you try you can build those barriers higher and higher until the department is all but isolated from the rest of the operation. In time this off-by-itself department can become so efficient that it will be above criticism. This is highly recommended for those readers who are content to stay where they are. It is a sure road to a dead end.

19

Some Autocrats of the Conference Table

THE LABOR-MANAGEMENT CONFERENCE is a book in itself; but whether or not you ever participate in a labor-management conference, there is one tactic in the art of conferring which you should sit down and learn from a union negotiator because you can use it every day of your life.

We have no interest for the moment in what you think of labor unions *or* management. The point is: when you're looking for instruction, go to the professionals. That applies to football, soldiering, salesmanship, and especially to conferring.

About the best you'll find for instructors in business will be some extremely capable advanced amateurs. But in the union negotiator you're looking at a pro.

The one we want you to learn from is Michael Bradshaw, automotive. He is the professional. And the one lesson to take from him is contained in his instructions to four shop men who were going to accompany him into a negotiation.

"Now I want you men to listen to me carefully. The papers I have just put into your hands are the present union contract. I want you to cancel any social engagements you have for the next six nights. Take home that contract for the next six nights . . ."

He was interrupted by one of the men who said, "Mike, we've already studied this contract. Been working under it for a year."

"I'm not asking you to *study* it," snapped Michael Bradshaw. "Nor am I asking you to work under it. *I'm telling you to memorize it!*"

The four shop men looked at each other. Bradshaw continued, "I mean memorize it so you can quote it back to anyone, starting from any point in it. And I don't mean just memorize the *sense* of it. I mean memorize also *every word in it*, and I *do* mean word for word!"

The men wore slightly put-upon expressions. But Bradshaw said, "There is no power in a meeting like knowing what you're talking about."

That's all.

In the meetings which ensued Bradshaw's men had an astounding poise that came from knowing—and knowing exactly—what they were talking about. It is a formidable, silent, reinforcing tower of strength which shows through at every turn in the meeting. There is no substitute for it.

In the meeting that you are going into tomorrow on the subject of next year's departmental budget, you can't see into the future, you may not be able to cope with the unexpected development which may enter the meeting, you may not be able to handle the new face which may appear at that meeting. But one thing you *can* do, *today*, which will give you a quiet, glacierlike strength at that table tomorrow: you can know *everything* there is to know about the budget under which you are *now* working. You can know it forward and backward. You can know it so that you needn't refer to a single scrap of paper. You can know it better than anyone else at that table. In the words of Bradshaw, "There is no power like knowing (If you want to put this book down right now to get ready for a meeting tomorrow, do it.) what you're talking about."

Let's take instruction from the unions once more. We ask neither your admiration nor your scorn for this tactic. Nor do we invite you to use it. We only say, "Look, the conference is not something to be slept through. It is a contest."

On Tuesday afternoon at four o'clock the management of a small eighty-man metal working shop in Chicago had finally reached a hard-fought agreement with the union negotiators. It was all new to the management. The union had just organized the shop. It was therefore new to the men in the plant also.

The agreement reached on Tuesday afternoon was essentially this: a six cent per hour raise across the board, fully paid hospitalization, forty hours, paid vacation.

Like any combatants after a hard fight, management and the labor representative had a respect for each other that night, and relaxation set in on both sides. There would be a few more meetings, but mostly for routine confirmation and phrasing of the conclusion just reached.

However, at the next step the labor negotiator was to bring with him some shop representatives of the new local union. The negotiator asked the company to keep the agreement confidential until Friday.

On Tuesday evening, somehow, word seemed to drift through the shop force that management's best offer was a five cent an hour increase, and nothing else.

On Wednesday morning, in the presence of five men from the shop, management was startled to be confronted by new and vigorous demands from the union negotiator with whom they had parted so amicably Tuesday afternoon. He acted as though nothing had been settled. He was suddenly talking about ten cents an hour across the board, and some new fringe benefits which had never even entered previous discussions.

Management, therefore, promptly dug in its heels, stiffened its neck and fought back. They said, "Six cents an hour across the board, full hospitalization, forty hours, paid vacation; and that's it . . . period."

The union organizer said, "This is disappointing to us. May I caucus for ten minutes in private with my men?"

"Go ahead."

They returned, talking eight cents an hour. Management caucused this time.

To shorten the story, there were three more days of meetings in which the whole contract seemed to be being battled line by line all over again.

But oddly enough, at five o'clock on Friday evening,

just in time for the good news to be out for the weekend, the union negotiator gave up abruptly. Oddly enough the place where he yielded was exactly at a six cent an hour increase, fully paid hospitalization, forty hours, paid vacation.

He had done his job by Tuesday afternoon, and it was a good job. But he had another selling job on his hands, namely to sell his own union members on the contract he had reached. He thought the best way to sell his own men was to give them a three-day taste of it.

We are not interested at the moment in what you think of his method. But it should alert you to study the motives of men around the conference table.

Is the argument always what it seems to be? Are you sometimes witnessing a windowdressing argument? The man who opposes you . . . does he really care so much about the point at contest? Or has he another mission? Can you perhaps allow him a public victory and privately carry your point? Is he feinting you out of position on an issue he intends to concede later anyhow? Does he want only the appearance of opposing you?

Examine carefully the axe he is grinding, examine his motives.

Once more from the unions, a lesson which applies to every conference on every subject. The strength of your voice at the table depends ultimately upon your private decision about consequences. A union leader who has privately determined that he will not call a strike, cannot talk very loud at the table. A union man who privately knows exactly where his last ditch is, how much he will concede before striking, speaks with authority which penetrates to every man at the table.

The same applies to you. Your last ditch may be a price above which you will not pay, a standard less than which you will not accept, a delay beyond which you won't wait. It is a last ditch. It's not anything you talk about at the table. It's only something you privately decide. Having decided where that point lies, it's unlikely you'll ever have to settle for that.

But having privately decided on an alternative gives you the strength of William Tell—who had already faced up to the worst that could happen and chose his alternative when he put the spare arrow in his belt.

Another professional conferrer is the lawyer. Take a lesson from him.

Take three afternoons of your time to go to one of the best schools in the country on conferring. The tuition is free. Here is how you do it.

Go to your county courthouse. Walk to the "assignment desk." There will probably be a large blackboard hanging there. Chalked on the board will be the numbers of each courtroom in the building. It will also give you the subject of the trials and the names of the judges and the attorneys.

If there is no blackboard, ask the officer at the desk what is being argued in each courtroom. He will be glad to tell you and if you explain that you want to witness the best arguing available, he'll guide you well. He will know which attorneys are considered most competent and which cases will best demonstrate the argument in action.

You will not have to worry about prying into private lives. There will be civil cases having to do with land, loans, and business problems.

And in three afternoons you will learn a very great deal about conferring. You will be watching professionals.

Rejoice at trouble.

You are sitting in a conference with your right elbow on the table; your head is resting in your hand. It is 4:30 and you have been here since 1:30. There is still no solution to the problem. Things are now tangled into a hopeless mess; you are tired, and there seems to be nothing but trouble.

Did you ever think that this is the best thing that could happen to you?

Your only opportunity to sell your product or your service to this group is if they are in trouble. Don't look for opportunity where everything is fine. It isn't there. Trouble is your fortune.

Lee Sherman Chadwick was a young engineer with the Perfection Stove Company in Ohio. One day he was called into the office of Francis Drury, president. In the office were four other men who constituted top management. They were all depressed.

The company was in the business of manufacturing oil stoves for the Standard Oil Company. Standard Oil then sold these stoves under their name from their oil wagons, obviously to build the market for fuel oil. The stoves were built to strict Standard Oil specifications. And it had been a nice business for Perfection Stove Company.

But on this day Mr. Drury handed a telegram to young Chadwick. His gesture was full of despair, and apparently the telegram needed no explanation.

It said, "Effective March first we will terminate our contract with you for stoves. Stop. Will require no more in future."

Chadwick looked around the room at the gloom. He studied the telegram again. Apparently he had been called to this meeting to decide how quickly they could shut down the works. Instead he said, "Gentlemen, I congratulate you!"

The sad expressions changed to scowls. "Just what do you mean by that!"

"I mean," said Chadwick, "that now you can manufacture your own stove in your own design and size and you can put your own name on it."

Some of the scowls began to fade.

Chadwick continued. "For once you will get out of the dangerous position of having only one customer. Now you can have many customers. And with your own name on the stove, people will know you're in business. This is the best thing that could happen."

In real trouble the man who brings to the conference a

message of hope—which he's obviously willing to back up with performance—will be given the keys to the place.

You will not be surprised to learn that young Chadwick became president of Perfection Stove Company and held the job for twenty-seven years.

Charles W. Perelle had a kind of reputation in industry as a wonder boy. And you might say he achieved this name almost entirely by looking for trouble. He has had several careers, but all of them had to do with finding trouble. Any production line that wouldn't work right was an invitation to prosperity for Perelle.

For example, when the ACF Brill Company was losing 2.1 million dollars a year, Perelle took over.

The plant had no assembly line. It employed 2,300 men to build ten buses in three shifts.

Perelle spent $10,150 to buy himself an assembly line and a winch to pull it. Shortly he had seven hundred men making ten buses in one shift and the Brill Company turned in a profit. But the point is, Perelle's career hinged on troubles.

So does yours. Your troubles may be your trumps.

If your presentation in conference involves the use of physical props of some kind, do yourself the favor of practicing once with this prop before the meeting, however briefly.

For example, you may be the well-respected president of a large group insurance company, but you can look like a refugee from the awkward squad if you've never

threaded up a motion picture projector before. Certainly
it's simple, and you'll have no trouble mastering it. But
you'll have plenty of trouble if you never try it until the
moment you want to show the film.

The same applies to a slide film projector or a sound
recorder. You will suddenly find that you have a larger
set of thumbs than you ever bought gloves for; but more
important you will be amazed at how ridiculous your
proposal sounds as you stand there tangled in three
thousand feet of crazy mixed-up celluloid footage.

Now, of course, you may have a bright young man
along to operate the equipment *for* you. That's fine, but
make sure *he* knows how to thread up the projector, and
not just any projector, but the very *same* projector which
will be used at the conference. Projectors are different.

Have him check also to see that there are spare fuses,
bulbs, drive belts.

On top of all this, give a few seconds of thought to how
you'll handle things if the equipment breaks down anyhow. This seems extremely elementary, but don't find
out the hard way how important it is.

We've seen these physical props overdone too. For
example, we witnessed one conference where the ar-
rangements were just too perfect for success. When the
conferees arrived there rested squarely beside each place
an ash tray, a package of cigarettes, a pad of paper and
a sharpened pencil. They were placed there by the man
who was presenting the proposal; better stated, he was
there to sell a project.

Now if you give a man a paper and a pencil, you've

obviously invited his comments—and you'll get them. Since you've been to so much trouble to invite his opinions, by gosh, he won't disappoint you. Now what is he going to write on that piece of paper? Is he going to write down, "This is excellent! We should buy it immediately!"

No, sir.

You have just set up some fine mechanics to convenience the customer in unselling himself, in writing, no less; to distract himself from your presentation while he writes; also you've given him a place to doodle away the attention you need so desperately.

20

Is This Conference Necessary?

Finding the Source of Influence

We once knew *a jobber salesman of pneumatic* equipment who used to pause in the middle of a sales pitch to a new customer and say to his prospect, "Say, have you got the authority to buy this stuff or do I have to see your boss?" This was not calculated to win friends, but it did influence people. More often than not he got a straight-forward answer.

If he was talking to the right man the poor fellow almost had to prove his authority by giving our friend an order. If, as often happened, he was talking to the wrong man the very brashness of the question invited a certain respect.

Our outspoken friend had developed a surefire protection against the world's greatest time consumer—talking to the wrong man.

Except at the very highest levels where the president of one outfit calls the president of another, American businessmen have developed a strange psychosis which could be called the oblique approach.

The sales manager of the Bojim Mattress Company would like very much to confer with the chief house-keeper of the Jones Hotels Corporation. He's been tipped off that they're building a new hotel in Kamchatka. For some inexplicable reason he never calls the Jones Hotel Corporation and asks to speak to the chief housekeeper. Instead, he calls in his assistants. "Any of you know anybody over at the Jones Hotels Corporation?" he asks. No one does, so he keeps on searching among his acquaintances. Finally, it turns out that the bartender at the Athletic Club has a cousin who knows the head bell-boy at the Jones Plaza. Wheels begin to turn within wheels. Nine or ten weeks later the sales manager of the Bojim Mattress Company finds himself face to face with the chief housekeeper of the Jones Hotels Corporation who, it turns out, has just last week placed an order for mattresses with Bojim's competitor.

This cycle of nobody talking to nobody is pursued with fiendish diligence and is known variously as "laying the groundwork," "getting the lay of the land," "developing a contact," "surveying the situation," "taking a reading," and so on, ad infinitum.

As many as half the sales conferences you will be called upon to attend (it happens more often in sales situations than anywhere else) may be devoted to laying out "strategy," which is to say, mapping the route from the bartender to the bellboy and on to the chief housekeeper.

We were present at a conference such as that some time ago where the strategic objective was an audience with Fred Crawford, who was at that time president of the great Thompson Products organization and the National Association of Manufacturers.

For two hours the conferees talked strategy. Many of them were acquainted with key men of the Thompson organization and a full-scale argument developed over which of these various "contacts" would provide the best route to Mr. Crawford.

Finally, the strategy was set; a man was assigned to get it underway. But something went wrong. In relaying his instructions he failed to make the strategy clear to one of the assistants. An hour later an emergency call went out for an immediate conference.

The blundering assistant had misunderstood. He'd called Thompson Products and asked to speak to Mr. Crawford who was more than glad to grant the interview.

The strange and wonderful thing about the man in authority is that he's almost never hard to reach. Moreover, if you have a sound proposition to make, he's actually anxious to hear it.

One of the great universal errors of these times is the assumption that some devious influence must be brought to bear in order to reach the man who makes the decisions.

How this peculiar state of affairs developed is difficult to track. Probably it developed because everybody prefers talk to action. And when we're not talking we have our "ear to the ground." This makes all of us as alert as a troop of Eagle Scouts on a bird walk. Whenever we pick up the slightest fragment of trade gossip we carry it, as on a velvet pillow, to the most important man in our circle, who immediately relays it to the most important man in his circle. In this manner we accumulate tremendous resources of misinformation which we consider vital to the conduct of our everyday business affairs.

The man who makes the most use of it is, of course, the man who has no power to make decisions. He has the power to call conferences, though, and he uses it freely.

This man of no authority is usually very difficult to see. But if you go by the bartender-bellhop route it can usually be arranged. You can then be prepared for a series of conferences. They will be full of sound and fury but they will signify nothing.

Many a conference is foredoomed to failure for the simple reason that the really influential factor is not among those present.

For example, if you sell steam boilers you can arrange a dozen conferences with the people who are putting up the money for the building. Ninety-nine times out of a hundred, though, the owners will not decide the make of boiler that will go into the building. The architect will. And even though you manage to sell the owners, you can depend upon it, the architect will unsell them if he wants to.

The real source of influence in a situation is often a subtle and elusive thing.

We know of one YMCA executive, for instance, who makes a practice of getting local big names to serve on his fund-raising committees. The individuals themselves would seem to be the source of influence, but our Y man knows better. Once he has obtained the consent of the civic leaders, he calls a luncheon meeting of their secretaries. After that he simply deals with the girls. His fund drives always go over the top.

A topnotch public relations man for one of this nation's most important industrial companies calls a meeting of the leading newspaper and magazine writers of the country. He makes his big presentation, but he knows these men hear similar reports from his competitors every day of their lives. So he goes to the source of influence. While the reporters are attending his meeting he sends a sample of his product as a gift to their wives, compliments of his company. Attached to it is the note, "Thanks for the loan of your husband."

The point is, in any conference, keep your eye on the real source of influence. It will save your time and energy which are all you have to sell.

21

Be Prepared

THERE WAS THIS BOY SCOUT who studied for months to be prepared for the overnight hike. He knew every lesson in the book. Besides the regular stuff, he took along a pith helmet, an extension cord, bicarbonate of soda, needle and thread, wire cutters, fire extinguisher and so on, until he was the most confident boy in the troop. The fact that he had to tote two packs instead of one was of no moment to him. A slight inconvenience, to be sure, but it was more than offset by the fact that he would be ready for any contingency.

This Boy Scout never finished the hike. Halfway out he broke his shoelace and he hadn't prepared for that.

This particular Boy Scout was the kind who thought the answer to this situation was to carry an extra pair of shoelaces around with him the rest of his life.

Despite this, the boy grew to manhood and because of his eye for detail and the orderly manner in which he went about everything, he rose to the rank of junior executive in a large corporation. One day the big boss

said to him, "Willis, that idea of yours for simplifying office procedure looks pretty good. I'm calling a conference about it next week. Be prepared to give us the whole story."

It was the biggest opportunity that had yet come Willis' way. He worked night and day on his presentation. He organized his thoughts and then organized the organizations. He rehearsed his presentation alone in a graveyard and then at home in front of his wife. When the big day came he was the most prepared junior executive who ever took the floor.

He had thought of everything. He started out with a chart showing the routing of a customer order. It got filed, Willis showed conclusively, in seventeen different departments, only four of which actually needed the information. He was doing splendidly, Willis was.

Now it happened that that morning the big boss's big boss had nicked himself while shaving. Willis' presentation of the seventeen departments made quite an impression on him. He stroked his chin when Willis pointed out that only four departments really needed to file the order. In doing this, he scratched the scab left by the razor nick. It started to bleed. He didn't notice it. But Willis did. Did it unnerve him? Not in the least. He was so well prepared nothing could unnerve him. The second part of his presentation, having to do with a simplified order form, got the boss stroking his chin again. He discovered his condition, but not until he'd smeared some of the blood on his shirt collar. He had a big appointment for lunch. He had to leave to go home for another shirt.

He instructed Willis to go right on with his story, he would have someone report to him.

That was some time ago. The customer orders are still being filed in seventeen places and Willis is still on his same old job.

No matter what they told you in high school, regardless of the lessons you learned at your mother's knee and in the fourth grade at Sunday school, DON'T BE TOO PREPARED.

If we had to choose between too little preparation or too much, we would a thousand times prefer the former. If you are underprepared you have, at least, your wits. If you are overprepared you have only your presentation.

One of the strangest and most interesting things about people is the fact that they change every instant of their lives. The person you were half an hour ago is not at all the same person you are now. Half an hour ago, had you been subjected to a given set of stimuli you'd have reacted one way. Right now you might react differently. We're not talking about any convictions you may have. If you abhor television now, no doubt you abhorred it half an hour ago too. But if your wife came in from working in the garden half an hour ago and you paid her no attention, chances are you'll put this book aside if she comes in now to show off her new negligee.

Every man who reports for a conference has necessarily left behind him several items of unfinished business. They can range from unfinished correspondence to an impending dentist's appointment; from trying to get the Barton shipment out on time to trying to remember whether Milwaukee is on daylight saving time.

In this conference you must fight these broken chains of action for every man's attention. The man who is an artist at conferring learns not only to keep alert to these competitors, but even to turn them to his own purpose.

Take Willis, for example; he had made his first point. It was time for a break in the intense continuity of his thought. The boss's scratched chin provided an excellent opportunity for a break. Had he said, "Mr. Jenkins, you seem to have nicked your chin . . ." Mr. Jenkins would have dabbed at it with his handkerchief, made some joke about it, and then when everything had settled down, Willis might have gone on to his next point and a better job. Had he been less prepared he probably would have, but Willis relied on his presentation, not his wits.

Like the mythical golfer who wets his finger to test the wind before addressing his ball, it is well to take a reading on the individuals around the conference table before plunging in. Most everyone does this automatically when he is conferring with strangers. An all too common error, however, is to assume that the old Jonesy of an hour ago is the same old Jonesy now. Jonesy may have had a hunk of good news in that hour, which has him riding a wave of confidence that makes him much more formidable. If you fail to notice this, you're overlooking a factor that can be turned to your advantage.

Between the time the boss asked you to get the facts together for a conference on that idea of his to pay the employees in cash instead of by check, he may have had his wallet stolen. It will be important that your presentation cover this possibility.

If you'll just think back at the labyrinth of loose ends

you leave unattended when you step into the conference
room and multiply your own by the number of persons
present, you begin to have some respect for the job
ahead of you, namely, capturing the undivided attention
of the members of the group.

No presentation, however elaborate or dramatic or
well rehearsed, can hope to overcome the little things
that make human being behave like, well, human beings.
This takes alertness, observation and wit.

We are not, of course, recommending that you come
into the conference drooling and stupid regarding the
subject at hand. We think you ought to know as much
about the subject as you possibly can. We think you
should have in mind a sequence for presenting your
information so that it will provide the greatest possible
impact. In fact you should be so well informed that you
can at an instant's notice abandon that sequence and
make up an entirely new one on the spot if the occasion
demands.

If you know your subject, relax. Observe the other
people, look for help, watch for temporary personal pit-
falls like the nick on Jenkins' face, or the fact that Allen
looks like you ought to give him a chance to go to the
washroom. Put yourself in Allen's place and figure where
your mind would be under the same circumstances.

The really prepared conferee is the one who knows his
subject so well that he can concentrate on the personal
factors that confront him and modify his presentation to
accommodate them.

22

Telephone Conference

Mr. Bell's little gadget can make you.

We do not call your attention to its electronic wonder. They haven't changed it that much since Mr. Bell first connected it. But that's just the point. The psychology of it hasn't changed either. Almost from the day Bell electrified the U. S. Senate with it, a set of attitudes surrounded this piece of bakelite which you can put to work for you.

But first, give yourself a surprise. Would you take a pencil . . . now . . . and in the blank space below just list, by last name and subject of conversation, all the phone calls that you've made or received today? Write small; you'll need the room:

Those are the ones you remember. Tomorrow anchor a sheet of paper under the phone and keep an accurate tally.

Those are conferences. A product or an idea or a reputation was bought or sold or rejected each time. There is no way to estimate how much of the world's work is done by phone; but some entire businesses are built around the telephone. Careers are made on the phone.

A smile won't come through the receiver, nor a wink nor a touch on the shoulder nor a handshake. Leadership and salesmanship by telephone must therefore be in the voice, inflection, words.

Now if you think we're about to go into a charm school on voice culture, you underestimate us. It's harder than that because like time-motion study or automation or any other industry-shaking concept, it's common sense.

When your phone rings, a man has walked into your office. Give him your undivided, undiluted attention exactly as if he had pulled up a chair opposite your desk.

If you let a man get into your office, he has a right to be there and you do not ignore him. If you let a phone call get past your switchboard, the caller has a right to your attention. Otherwise arrange to screen out such calls. There is no law requiring a man to answer his telephone.

Then once the call gets in, drop that pencil, forget the other men in your office. Listen to him with your whole mind, and answer likewise. That is what is required to get across on the telephone. It is the very same old science of keeping your eye on the ball, only this time it's for money.

It is truer still if you are the one placing the call. You are entitled to the same concentrated attention from the other end of the wire. But you may have to demand it.

If you have been in this man's office at one time or another, put yourself there mentally now. Is he the kind who hunches the phone to his ear with his shoulder and continues working while he talks?

Josh him out of it. "Look, Ed, I know you. You're signing letters and writing memos while you're listening to me. Now, darn it, put that junk down a minute. And listen while I make you rich."

He'll probably laugh and give you his good ear.

Or is his office incessantly in conference so that he probably has a meeting going on right now, which will temper his attitude toward your call, or make his answers guarded? Don't try to guess. Ask him, "Ed, do you have a meeting going on? This is important, so call me back when you're through."

There's an extra advantage in this sometimes, too, depending on your mission, of course. But often you rouse his curiosity or interest so that he builds up a certain suspense and concentration about your call. By the time he calls you back, he's anxious to hear your message. Of course it works the other way too. It gives him time to think of defensive answers or excuses if he can guess your purpose. You have to decide about this.

But the point is, visualize the other man's position

when he takes your call, his surroundings, his problems. Is he the kind who gives you only half an ear even in your presence, while his eyes rove over the crowd or check every passerby in the hall? Then bolt his attention at the beginning of the call with short, direct statements of your case, or questions which require short answers.

Or is this the situation? Many times a secretary, meaning to help you, will track your man all over the building. If he has gone into another man's office, she may relay your call to him there. This is efficient and courteous. But if Ed is in his division manager's office, your call may handicap him. In any event, Ed will probably not be as much at ease on another man's phone as on his own.

If you sense this, let him off the wire. "Ed, I know you're not on your own phone. Call me back."

An almost sure clue that your man is not in a convenient position is if he uses the word, "yes." Observe on your telephone tomorrow how seldom a man uses the word "yes" colloquially. You'll find almost every other affirmative, "sure," "yeah," "uh-huh," "all right," "O.K.," "um-hm"; but seldom will a man in comfortable circumstances pronounce the explicit word, "yes." But he does use it when he's in a strange office, when he's harassed, when he wishes no one else to understand his conversation, when he wishes to conceal emotion in the shortest, most aloof possible answer.

When you hear the explicit, carefully pronounced, concise "yes," see if anything is wrong and what can be done about it.

A telephone gives you certain powers. It allows you to set the pace. It is something like a mirror.

You can get back the same mood or attitude or decisiveness that you deliver into that mouthpiece. And you can do this more markedly than you can in a face-to-face conference.

For example, suppose you are dealing with a man who postpones decisions, who finds it distasteful to decide right now, who likes to mull over a proposition until the last ounce of inspiration is gone out of it, the man who much prefers to write you a letter later about it. But you need action now, or an action-type attitude. This is a perfect mission for the telephone.

You can generate this attitude in him in direct reflection of your own.

If your own voice on the phone is brisk, statements short, questions direct, clipped—his will be too. Try it.

The only requirement on your part is a few seconds of preparatory thinking before you dial to organize your talk right down the line.

Thomas Doane is a sales manager of a large firm in Ohio which markets nationally. When he calls you on the phone you have two strikes on you before you start. First he's a big, genuinely friendly, quick-witted Irishman. Second, he knows precisely what he is going to say or ask, and if that leaves you a choice, he knows exactly what he's going to say next, whichever way you answer.

He sweeps in over the wire like a fresh wind out of Belfast. He states his business or asks his question and before you've lighted your cigarette he's waiting for your answer in a dead silence that prods you in the back to match his vigor. But he doesn't wait long. To match his decisiveness and dispatch you chuck down the cigarette, lean into the phone with your brain alive and working on all eight cylinders. Just about the time you're feeling good because you've caught up to him, you hear a most pleasant and infectious goodby and a click. There's a hole left in the room as broad as Doane's shoulders, and you're sitting there looking at the receiver as though the line were cut.

But the main point, next time he calls you're alert as soon as the switchboard says, "Mr. Doane on the line." It's like that famous Mr. Robinson who called, left his card, and departed before the butlers could announce, "Jack Robinson." But everywhere Doane goes, he gets top attention, I should say *concentration*.

Paul Uniak, advertising manager of Cleveland Diesel Division of General Motors, is another of the same kind.

You want to make an appointment with him. Usually in such cases there's a little palaver about time, place and purpose. With Uniak the conversation goes like this on his end:

"Fine. About what?"

"Good. Where?"

"All right. What time?"

"Fine. So long."

You're a little out of breath and you think you must have left some loose ends. But when you analyze it, everything is covered. And when you go to see him, you usually make sure you're organized. Saves a lot of his time and gets action.

Herb and Frank Hoover, of The Hoover Company, were two more of the same. And they got enough results so that today the Hoover "beats as it sweeps as it cleans" all over the world.

Now we said that around the telephone there are still certain original attitudes which will work for you. One of these is that a long distance call is important.

Obviously this has been diluted by time and familiarity. Yet on all levels it still works so well that it is hard to find a man whose time and attention you cannot command by the simple act of dialing "O."

From Cleveland to San Francisco, for three minutes, it costs $3.30 plus tax. And that is perhaps the biggest bargain on the industrial market today.

No matter what altitude of executive level you're calling, the very fact of your toll call tells the recipient two things about your message:

1) It needs an answer faster than the mail will furnish. Therefore urgent, at least to you.

2) Though you may presume upon three minutes of his time, you are willing to lay $3.30 cash on the line for it, which values his time at $156,000 per working year, which insults very few men.

Most men will talk to you on those terms. Further, they'll give you close attention and think fast because even the giants of industry remember their boyhood days when you talked fast and hushed up the whole house for a long distance call because the meter was ticking down at the phone company.

If you're selling in a competitive field, the long distance call to arrange a meeting or to make a point lifts you a notch out of the crowd. If you're buying, the long distance call gets you the supplier's close attention.

If you're instructing assistants, the long distance call sharpens their reception and rivets their attention. If you're requesting budget or authority or project approval from upstairs, the toll call gets decision.

In fact, it works so well that a printing salesman of our acquaintance often waits until he goes *out* of town to make certain calls back to his *home* town.

On the way home from work last night and on the way down this morning, you've thought of several people you want to call today. Make those calls as soon as you get into the office . . . first thing.

The plain physiology of it is that seven hours' sleep have put you in the best shape you'll be in all day. More important, the recipient of your call is in the best shape he'll be in all day. The crisis he left on his desk last night doesn't look so bad this morning.

Both parties are still relaxed. Nature's morning shine still decorates this old earth. Your friend's phone is not yet steaming. The very hour of your call invests you with some of the freshness and aggressiveness of the early bird.

You get the callee's first and best attention of the day.

If you postpone the calls to midmorning they lose some of the boldness that comes with ideas conceived at night. You get bogged down in your day's routine, and it's the out-of-routine moves that make the lightning strike.

If you don't place those calls first off, you're apt to postpone them until the end of the day. But when the end of the day approaches, they don't look so good to you, and they look worse than that to the recipient who is trying to close down his shop for the day and does not want to open up any new major projects. Even if he were willing, there is no time left today to do anything about your call.

After 3:00 P.M., the chances are the man on the other end of the wire just wants to get today's sawdust swept up by quitting time. A new idea, a new project makes him tired and you are a buzz in his bad ear.

Now about this game of pussyfoot on who shall come to the phone first . . . it's for the little leagues.

John Murphy, president of The Higbee Company, one of the large department stores of the country, answers his own phone. Wendell Willkie did the same.

Now perhaps that's extreme and inconvenient for your particular case. So take whatever precautions are honestly necessary for your own efficiency. But frankly, the following coy little charade has been laughed out of business:

MISS MOORE: Mr. Little would like to talk to Mr. Smaller.

MISS MILLER: Mr. Smaller, Mr. Little would like to talk to you.

SMALLER: Is Mr. Little on the wire?

MISS MILLER: Miss Moore, is your party on the wire?

MISS MOORE: Mr. Little, I have Mr. Smaller's office for you.

LITTLE: Good. Hello, Mr. Smaller? Oh . . . who's this?

MISS MILLER: Just a minute, sir. I'll connect you. (*Click*) Mr. Smaller, Mr. Little to talk to you.

LITTLE: Hello, Smaller? This is Little.

That's right. It is. And it's getting smaller every day, thank goodness. Secretaries have developed a private little classification system: big shots, middle shots, and beebee shots, the latter being recognizable because they wear the oversize clothes of the former. The real brass they quickly recognize by forthright, common ordinary gentlemanliness, the gentleness that comes with strength.

23

Who Are You Working For?

Now we'd like to take up a subject of serious import
to the rising young executive as well as to his company
management. It has a real and direct influence on the
attitudes of people around the conference table.

The conference, after all, is an assembly of attitudes.
Every man around the table has brought an attitude with
him. Even the man who claims to be open-minded on a
subject, never is. Usually the man who talks loudest
about this open-mindedness is the man with the most
preconceived notions. And even if this protester of
innocence actually is open-minded, he has brought *that*
attitude to the conference table.

In conferring, as we have indicated earlier, it is important to measure the attitude of every man present, not
only toward the problem at hand, but, much more important, every man's attitude toward the company itself.

Here's a little exercise that will demonstrate the importance of what we have to say on this subject. Run

down the names of your associates and classify them as either "company" men or "other."

Probably you know already what we mean. Jonesy, the old reliable "beyond the call of duty" is, of course, "company." He has a bland, settled, all-in-a-day's work demeanor that management says is a good stabilizing influence on the younger people. One look at Jonesy and a perfect stranger could at once peg him as "company." He has long since made his peace with Mammon, that is to say, he has anticipated his income for years to come and has learned to regulate his tastes so they never outrun it.

Now Smitty, on the other hand, would have to be classified as "other." He has recently graduated from Chevrolet to the light model Buick. He also holds the opinion that anyone who drives a Cadillac is either a phony or an old fogey. Smitty works long and hard and talks a lot about it. He's liable to know more about company affairs, particularly those in other departments, than even old Jonesy does. Smitty is particularly popular with visiting salesmen. He has quite a following among the younger men in the districts.

Smitty, in other words, is on the make. He figures someday somebody else in the same business might be able to use a fellow with his experience, or maybe, if things break just right, he'll take over a territory himself; maybe even set up a little shop of his own.

Now between Jonesy and Smitty, the two easily recognized extremes in this matter of attitudes, are infinite variations of loyalty to self and loyalty to company.

Now, we hasten to add, we have *no* interest in the morals of this question. We are interested in exploring with you only the efficiencies of it. The morals, it seems to us, are about equally questionable. When the company hires a bright young man, it hopes to develop him into a corporate asset. The young man has no less right to turn the company into a personal asset if he can.

Now, if you have classified the more obvious men around you, how about yourself? Are you "company" or "other"?

That, sir, is about the most important question career-wise you will ever ask yourself.

Let's go back for a moment to the day you came to work for your present company. Remember how rosy the prospects seemed to you? Remember how you came home those first nights and told about your manager and his manager? Remember how you figured it was a good business to be in because somebody always needed the product, etc., etc.?

Then the glow wore off. The manager became a nice guy but lacked vision. Already you had your eye on a couple of changes that would make big improvements, if you just had the chance to bring 'em to the attention of the proper people. Then you began developing the proper people. In the conferences you made sure you looked good. First thing you knew, you were upgraded and that became a new plateau from which to repeat the process.

Now in those conferences in which you were developing the proper people, did you have your eye on the ball?

That is, was your full attention directed to the matter at hand?

Of course it wasn't. The conference was an opportunity to progress in the direction that seemed advantageous to you, regardless of whether the immediate problem was solved.

Now, we're not getting moral. If you sabotaged the whole effort and ended up a vice president, more power to you. All we're asking you to admit is that this kind of thought process, or something close to it, *did* go on in that scheming brain of yours. We want you to admit it because, if it did, you can be more valuable to the company or to yourself, whichever side of the fence you elect to jump.

You can no more remain half slave and half free than this nation could and it's time you were resolving that little war that's going on inside you.

Just in case you don't know it, although you probably do, most of the people around you are wrestling with this same decision. That's particularly true of your nearest competitor. He's even careful to be nice to you because in the back of his mind he's thinking he might need you someday.

One of you is going to come out on top. It will almost inevitably be the one who first gets straight in his mind who he's working for—himself or the company.

As long as you are promoting your own career first and the company's interest second you are, in effect, running your own little business at the expense of the company. You may be very clever at it, but prepare yourself for a shock—everybody knows your secret.

Your associates know it, the visiting salesmen know it, the men in the territory know it, and even the big brass, such of it as is aware of you, knows it too. You've been carrying a terrific burden, you see.

Now if you've made up your mind to stay with the present outfit only long enough to gain experience or capital or acquaintances enough to strike out for yourself, go on to the next subject. You're all set.

But if you still have one foot in each of these canoes, you can use some advice.

The first thing you have to do is get rid of that burden you've been carrying. Now that's going to be tough— like deciding to marry the girl when you don't love her.

You probably don't know it, but that indecision of yours has been your escape from the routine boredom and the irritation of your job. When things got tough you wandered off into that pleasant world of yours where you were the boss, where all the decisions were your decisions. Where you called the plays and the rest of the team followed your orders. It was easy to conjure up that dream because, you told yourself, it's really partly true already. Why, every day in every way you're growing more and more independent of these people who make your life so miserable. With just a little more money or experience you'll be able to tell the whole outfit where to head in—show 'em a thing or two.

Now if you decide that your career is with the company you've got to give up all that pleasantness. You've got to decide that come hell or high water you're stuck with it. There's no escape for you except in company channels. You've got to marry the girl until death do ye part.

This is a matter of discipline and that's never easy to come by, particularly when you can't browbeat the subject. It comes easier when you look at the rewards. The day you make up your mind to think "company" everyone will know it. The people around you will know it, the visiting salesmen will know it, the men in the districts will know it, and the big brass will know it.

The visiting salesmen are likely to change their attitudes the quickest. They find out you don't work for the company, you *are* the company. With the full corporate weight of the company behind you, you're pretty formidable. You'll find them selling harder. They'll be talking more about what their product can do for your company, and less about the trade gossip that you were always so eager to hear.

Before, they could handle you. They could imply that they knew a good spot for a guy like you if the time ever came, etc. Now, though, in the light of your new determination to work for the company, you're a much tougher prospect than you were before. And if you prove out, the things they'll say about you in other places is what you always hoped they were saying before, only they weren't.

And the men in the field . . . once the new attitude reaches them, you might change your mind about all the things you thought were wrong with the company.

You'll find there are some pretty good men on the payroll. They won't be so quick to put the bar check on *their* expense account the next time you're in town, but they'll be trying to get your ear and that's even more flattering.

You'll suddenly find yourself with a lot more weight in the conferences. You'll become formidable. A lot of the talk will turn in your direction, and the big brass will be quick to notice. You don't work *for* the company; you *are* the company.

The biggest reward, though, will come in the peace of mind and the directness of purpose such a decision will bring about. That in itself will contribute mightily to putting you where you want to be. Who are the really strong men in your company? Is there any doubt in your mind who they'll be working for a year from now? That's the greater part of their strength.

You can build a big career inside the company, but not until you shut the door of that fire escape you've been running down whenever things didn't suit you.

Suppose now that your decision went the other way. You make up your mind that, while you're not ready just yet to quit the company, you're definitely not going to marry it.

Now you can put the visiting salesmen to really good use. You can get a line on the whole field.

And the men in the field—now you can cultivate the best of them with an eye on the day they'll be useful to you.

You can poke around in other departments, learn

phases of the business you never knew about before.

Of course, you can't do this very long. But you can put the time to good use.

The point is, get on one side or the other and go. Chances are you can make a go of it either way.

The only thing that will deprive you of your chance to find out is that gnawing indecision, that pain in the stomach that comes from sitting out your life on the fence.

24

The Irate Delegation

. . . how to handle the "citizens and taxpayers"

In the political arena, no less than in business, conferences make the world go round. We have nothing to say
to the professional conferees around the table at the
United Nations, nor to the professionals of the "smoke-
filled room." These career men of the conference have
rules all their own which have little application outside
the ranks of the pros.

But there are countless situations where Joe Taxpayer
finds himself involved in community affairs, which is to
say, conferences.

Where is the man so alert that he has not at some time
or other awakened to find himself on the stunt night committee of the PTA? Where is the taxpayer who has never
found it necessary to protest an action of the Zoning
Board or the City Council or the Board of Education?
If these things have not yet befallen you, you are very
young. Read on. They will.

Sooner or later someone will want to put up a low quality house in the heart of your neighborhood. Inevitably as tomorrow, the garbage man will skip your block; teenage hot rodders will roar through your nights; a do-good crusader will introduce a tax levy for a municipal Turkish bath. When these things happen, you will be forced into the community conference and you'd better know how to go about it.

To get at this subject, let us take up a non-hypothetical situation involving a typical community crisis.

Here's the situation:

The School Board of a fine residential suburban community has announced plans to build a new elementary school on land which it acquired some years before. It's an ideal site, centrally located, surrounded by new homes.

Everybody knows the school is needed, so the bond levy passes easily. Plans are drawn, contracts let and everything's ready to go. One night at a PTA meeting the school superintendent brings out an architect's drawing of the new school. It meets with general approval. But then a bright young successful businessman whose home overlooks the site notices something. The back of the school faces his property. All the time he thought the back of the school would face the guys across the street.

His face darkens, his hands clench. He leaves the meeting to hurry home and man the telephone. In a matter of minutes (where their rights are involved, taxpayers will drop anything) all the neighbors whose houses will also face the back of the school are assembled in his recreation room, *their* faces grim, *their* hands clenched.

The first of several community conferences is underway.

Four points of view will rapidly evolve from this situation: The point of view of the back-of-the-school tax-payers; the point of view of the front-of-the-school tax-payers; the point of view of the once-removed taxpayers who live one street or more away from the school; and last, the point of view of the members of the Board of Education, around whom the storm will center as the democratic process gets underway.

Let us now join the recreation room conferences of the back-of-the-school group. We are incensed. Our rights as citizens and taxpayers are at stake. This thing threatens the value of our homes. Our view will be wiped out. A bunch of noisy kids will be screaming and shouting in our front yards from morning until night. Cars will be parked on the street in front of our houses. If we'd known they were going to do a thing like this we never would have bought here in the first place. We don't have to put up with this; after all, we're citizens and taxpayers.

Indignation will reach a white heat. There will be a lawyer in the crowd and he will propose legal action. We will all listen as he outlines our case. An older man will suggest that legal action be held in abeyance. First, he suggests we should organize a protest meeting to make our feelings known to the members of the Board of Education. Someone will ask who's on the Board of Education and no one will know for sure. Finally, it will be discovered that one of the members is a friend of somebody on the Board. We will commission him to talk the matter over privately with this friend, get the lay of the land and report back to this group. This will end conference number one, although the indignation talk will go on in smaller groups most of the night.

A week passes and the word gets out that the back-of-the-school group is organizing to get the school turned around. Let us now join the conference of the front-of-the-school group. This will also occur in a recreation room.

Here our attitudes will be more reasonable. After all, someone will point out, we bought our homes knowing they were adjacent to school property. We took the same chance that the back of the school might face our side. The Board of Education no doubt has excellent reasons for facing the building as it did.

A committee will be formed to observe the actions of the back-of-the-school people. If they seem to make any headway this committee will spread the alarm to all of us in the front-of-the-school sector. This conference will drift into relatively calm discussion groups whose principal topic will be the generally undesirable characteristics of those people across the way. Enthusiasm for this subject will mount with each new anecdote and we will adjourn to our respective homes rather thankful that the new school will separate us from this low element.

Now let us move our point of view to the once-removed group one street or more away from the proposed building. Here there will be no formal conference. We will discuss the situation calmly and reasonably with our neighbors. We will come to the conclusion that people certainly can be unreasonable.

For the moment we will not put ourselves in the place of the Board of Education members, we'll come to that in due course.

Instead, let us join the back-of-the-school group in conference number three, the protest meeting at the Board of Education.

We are well organized. We have chosen a spokesman who will voice our protest. The rest of us will chime in later, depending upon how everything goes. We have agreed to be as reasonable as possible with the Board, but to put up with no nonsense.

As we file into the Board room for our conference we find it hard to maintain our reasonable attitude. There they sit, the five bureaucrats who had no more sense of social responsibility than to destroy the value of our homes with this arbitrary and irresponsible action. Our feelings are in no way soothed, either, when we notice a bunch of those front-of-the-school people on hand to spy on us.

This is a regular meeting of the Board (we were advised by our friend's friend not to ask for a special meeting to voice our protest). We expect, considering the import of our business, that we'll be first on the agenda. But no. The Board president is calling for a treasurer's report. That takes forty-five minutes. A lot of gobbledy-gook about teachers' pay rolls, the cost of textbooks, the problem of whether or not to buy snow plow attachments for the schools' tractors.

That's over finally, now they'll get to us. But no. They're considering written communications. Somebody wants to use the high school auditorium to put on an Evangelist meeting. Somebody wants the Board to provide home tutoring for a crippled child. A group of people, obviously selfish, want to know why the school bus can't come down their street and pick up the kids at their doorsteps, instead of making them all walk to the one bus stop. Things like that take up another half hour and by this time we're burning up. Obviously, they mean to flaunt their authority in our faces . . . make us sit here through all this trivia. Well, just wait. Sooner or later they've got to face it.

Now before this crucial conference begins, let us place ourselves in the position of the president of this Board of Education. In the first place, he is not a politician. This Board job pays no money, requires a lot of time and infinite patience. There's no reward connected with it except the satisfaction of doing a job that has to be done. Meetings are supposed to be confined to one a month, but they average one a week. This man has served on the Board for six years. He's wrestled with problems he never thought could exist. He's a custodian of mops and books and real estate. He's a hirer of teachers, a selecter of boiler plants, a buyer of food, an arbiter of disputes. He has to be something of a lawyer, an architect, a tax expert, a psychologist and, above all, an expert conferrer

He knows that an irate delegation is present this night,

but he's used to irate delegations, he seldom gets a chance to deal with any other kind. He lets them sit through most of the routine business hoping against hope that they might get the idea that their problem is only one of many the Board faces. This man, we said, is a veteran of the conference. There is much to be learned from his subsequent handling of this one.

"We come now to oral petitions," the Board president says pleasantly. "I believe we have a delegation from Meadow Lane Avenue who would like to discuss plans for our new elementary building. Who would like to speak first for your group?"

The spokesman for our back-of-the-school group gets to his feet. He seems a little nervous, gets off to a rather timid start. But as he gets used to it he warms up. He explains about how we all worked all our lives to own these homes only to see their value destroyed now by this ill-considered placement of a school building. His voice grows emotional as he develops this theme and the rest of us can hardly resist the impulse to add more to what he is saying. Our spokesman ends up with an eloquent appeal that the Board reconsider its decision in the light of the hardship it will work on all of us. He sits down and there's silence in the room. We expect the president to defend the Board's decision now, but he doesn't. He just says, "Thank you, sir. Who's the next speaker for your group?"

We hadn't planned for the next speaker, but a lot of us were ready to carry on. Three of us start talking at once. The president says there's plenty of time for everyone to be heard and singles out one of us to go on. He does. He says the same things, adding only that we're citizens and taxpayers and intend to stand up for our rights.

The Board president goes on, inviting everybody to have his say.

For forty-five minutes we go on. But the longer we talk, the less steam there seems to be behind our speeches. Then we wise up all at once. He wants us to talk ourselves out, then he'll defend the Board decision. He asks if anyone else would like to be heard. But we're wise to him now. We shut up. Now it's his turn.

He says, "I want you to know we appreciate your coming here to explain your point of view on this matter. It is of course, a serious matter to all of us. I'd like to compliment you folks on the reasonable manner in which you've approached the problem. I know you'll want us to decide this thing in the best interests of the children and I can assure you we will do that to the best of our ability."

Well, he thought he'd dismiss us as easy as that. But we weren't in any mood to listen to bureaucratic soft soap. "What are you going to do about it?" one of our people demanded.

"We're not going to take up the subject tonight," the president said. "We have too many other things to consider. Perhaps, though, you folks would like to have a copy of the site plans for the school. Maybe you could come in later with a suggestion that would solve everybody's problem."

One of the front-of-the-school delegates spoke up then. "We'd like a copy of those plans, too," he said.

The clerk handed out copies to both sides and we left. We had to admit afterward that the Board was quite reasonable about the whole thing.

How did it end? Well, we got into a big fight with the people across the street who were the real culprits. After all, the school had to be built. It had to face some direction.

Besides, they've planted a row of high shrubs along the back line of the school which looks very nice from our front porches.

Right behind the bushes they've built a parking lot which serves the double purpose of keeping the cars from parking in front of our houses, and moves the playground far enough away so the children don't bother us.

What did the school board president say in handling this irate delegation?

Nothing. He listened.

To you, Mr. Reader, we have this to say. In the community conference beware of the words "Citizen and Taxpayer." They imply that the people on the other side of the argument are neither.

Suggestion number two: Don't wait until you face a personal crisis to find out what goes on in your home town. The important things are decided in hundreds of conferences at which every citizen and every taxpayer is more than welcome. It takes up your time, of course, to attend them, but a lot of good citizens are giving up their time to arrive at the decisions. If you show up after they're made and sound off about your rights as a citizen someone is likely to tell you to shut up, and he will be right.

If you ever sit on the other side of the conference table, as the councilman or the school board member, or the chairman of the PTA stunt-night committee, your success will be proportional to your ability to absorb the fury of the scorned citizen and turn it into support. It can be done, but never by a frontal attack. Treat unreasonableness as though it were sweetly reasonable. If you can't master this technique don't run for office, on the City Council, the Board of Education, or, for that matter, as counsellor to the Women's Executive Board of the Meadow Lane Brownie Pack. These offices require statesmanship, which is to say, the ability to lose the argument and win the conference.

25

Man the Lookouts

FRED GYMER, a young fellow we know who invents cockeyed philosophical slogans for the business world and sells them successfully, has one appropriate to what we have to say now.

It reads:

> IF YOU CAN KEEP YOUR HEAD WHEN
> ALL ABOUT YOU ARE LOSING THEIRS
> IT MAY BE THAT YOU JUST DON'T UN-
> DERSTAND THE SITUATION.

Conferences are being lost every day because the principals fail to understand the situation. We saw that happen on a high level not long ago.

The conference had been called by a vice president. There was actually no decision to be made; it had been made already in the V.P.'s mind. To get the team behind him, however, he felt the politic thing to do was to call a conference, review the facts, and steer events so that his personal decision would seem like a conference decision.

At first everything went well. The V.P. let the boys talk themselves out. This began to get very dull but he prided himself on his patience. He stifled a few yawns and let it go on. Fatigue began to take over; tempers flared; prejudices crept in. The V.P. began to be irritated himself, but he kept his head. He rapped for order.

"This thing has gone far enough," he said. "The Sullivan plan for district reorganization goes into effect tomorrow morning."

The sales manager, without whom the plan couldn't possibly succeed, spoke up. "If it goes in its present form you can find yourself another boy," he snapped.

The district coordinator who thought he ought to be sales manager chimed in, "Look who's handing out ultimatums—well, I got one of my own. If the Sullivan plan doesn't go in . . ."

The V.P. drowned them both out. "Nobody's issuing ultimatums around here, not even me. We'll work on this thing some more. I'll call you together again in a few days."

The vice president had come to his senses just in time. In the course of the conference he had neglected to man the lookouts. There were plenty of warnings that fatigue, impatience and prejudice had taken over. He had simply failed to observe them.

To have pressed his decision further at that time would have been disastrous. There was only one thing left to do, break up the conference and start off on a new tack.

There would have to be conferences with the key individuals, a lot of giving and taking, a lot of selling and salving. Not until he had established a common denominator of acceptance for the Sullivan plan would he dare call this same conference again.

How do you recognize the warning signals that foretell when a conference is heading for trouble?

The best indicator is yourself. If you're stifling a yawn, chances are others are, too. If one of the conferees, who at first seemed to have a tolerable—if misdirected—point of view begins to look like a fat ignoramus, watch out. To him you're beginning to look like a stubborn alligator.

If you started the conference recognizing every man's right to his own point of view and later find yourself remembering that this guy doing all the talking is from Notre Dame and therefore not to be trusted, watch out. He's remembering that you don't like to ride airplanes.

If the subject of the conference seemed of real importance earlier and now seems less vital than your luncheon date, watch out. Its importance is decreasing in everyone else's perspective, too.

Be alert to the warning signs right from the beginning of the conference, in fact, even before it begins.

In a recent situation which happens all too often, a little preconference investigation might have avoided what turned out to be an unsuccessful sales pitch. The conference was set for the late afternoon because one of the principal figures in the sale had another meeting in the morning. In this morning meeting, however, this Mr. Big was himself selling something.

Things went badly for him. He failed to make his sale. Saddle-sore from this defeat as a seller he walks into conference number two in which he is the *buyer*. A bigger man could have left his personal defeat at the doorway of the afternoon conference, but these "bigger" men are, unfortunately, rarer birds than you would imagine from all the titles you see on the corporation doorways.

Touch Every Base

There's another way of heading off the danger signs in a conference before they happen.

Ted Fowler, who is an expert at it, calls it "touching every base." One man in history made a reputation by *not* touching second base. But thousands of men are daily achieving oblivion by not touching every base.

Fowler is with a big company which you'd recognize instantly. We'd rather not mention it because it might destroy his ability to continue using his system, and he's headed for big things.

But his management is very conservative and very effective. Over the years their batting average for smart decisions has made their trademark the symbol for their whole industry. They're slow to take up a new method because the ones they're now using are obviously good. But when they do decide to adopt a new course of action or plan of attack, they do it big. It takes an enormous amount of internal selling, though.

Now in this ultraconservative organization Fowler has a high average for getting his plans pushed up through all echelons to completion. And to watch Fowler sell a project all the way up to and through three floors in the marble tower is drama.

First off, Fowler mostly seems to listen. From a round face a pair of blue eyes peer at you intently and respectfully from behind fairly thick lenses. His head nods, confirming your remarks as you go along. Occasionally his round face breaks into a crinkled network of smiles that light up the room. Occasionally he inserts a slight joke into the conversation and grins experimentally, hoping you like it. Everybody does, and then he's consumed with modest gratitude that you should find it so funny.

He never speaks loudly. He does not seem to be trying to sell you a project. In fact he only seems to be asking your advice. But before you wake up to the fact that this advice seeker is in the middle of a long-range campaign, you find that you have already added your name to the list of people in favor of the project. He has done it in a way that would make it most awkward for you to retract later.

But this is all preliminary. Ted Fowler's secret is the broadness of the base he builds under his project. And he builds from the bottom.

Fowler's ideas are all big. They usually require Board of Director action. But Ted is eight floors below the Board. Between him and the Board are several floors of top management. But Fowler at first makes no attempt to get the ear of anyone way upstairs.

He begins on his own floor, and even a couple floors below him. Patiently he begins to march his project upstairs, never going over anyone's head, never crossing any wires or pulling any. And as he marches slowly up he collects behind him—perhaps we should say *ahead* of him—such an aggregation of support that from a director's view it must look as though all management is clamoring for Ted's project. Ted Fowler himself? Well, they never heard of him. In fact, when the big showdown comes he may not even be invited to the meeting.

He begins by making a list of what he calls "all the bases that must be touched."

Sales Mgr. .... Johnson
Ad. Mgr. .... Miller
Industrial Relations .... Cox
Production Mgr. .... Jones
Research Dir. .... Blaw

We said, "But, Ted, your project doesn't concern all those departments. Why give them a voice in it?"

"Any project that's worth this much trouble and costs this much money affects all departments," Fowler said.

"Yes. But you could go straight up through your own specialty channel. You don't have to ask production and industrial relations what they think."

"No. Don't *have* to," Fowler said. "But at the top level any idea requiring funds is competing for those funds with requisitions from the other departments."

"Yes, but you could let that competition be settled by the Board. *You* don't have to fight all the other departments to get your funds."

"Don't want to fight them for the money," Fowler grinned. "Want them to force it upon me."

With his initial list of bases to be touched, Fowler

begins making the rounds in his quiet way, testing his idea out on these men . . . e-a-s-y does it. It looks like he doesn't care too much one way or the other at first. He casually points out why the idea would be good for their departments. He naturally gets some kind of reaction from each. He asks them how they would execute it, and in answering this question they are selling themselves on it. "Why, if I had that in my hands today," says the sales manager, "I'd use it on that hidebound customer of ours in Boston, for example!"

Fowler lets them build themselves into it.

Now he goes back to his office. He's done well so far. But these men may forget. They may change their minds. They may be promoted or absent when he needs their vote at showdown time.

Now he adds to the list:

Sales Mgr.	Johnson
1st Ass't.	McDonald
2nd Ass't.	Ewing
Ad. Mgr.	Miller
Ass't.	Peele
Industrial Relations	Cox
Ass't.	Perry
Production Mgr.	Jones
Ass't.	Bleem
Ass't.	Norris
Research Dir.	Blaw
Ass't.	Higgins

Now he goes back over the ground. And to the assistant he can say, "Say, did Johnson tell you about the new plan?"

"Uh, yeah. Said something about it. No details."

"Well, he seemed quite enthusiastic about it. Like to fill you in on the details, and see what you think."

He fills in the chinks by selling the assistants on the idea. Fowler says this is important.

The boss may like the idea, but if one of his assistants spikes it with sarcasm, and if the assistant is worth his salt, the boss will listen and cool off quick.

Notice the advantage now when he calls on the research director's assistant. He modestly prefaces his remarks by, "Mr. Blaw seemed to like the idea. But I thought I'd like to check it out with you in more detail. Then you can pick the time to tell Mr. Blaw more of the details, and see he doesn't forget."

Higgins is now included in an important way. He has a mission in it, therefore an interest. It will not come to him as a surprise, which he can resent.

Ted Fowler patiently works his way all around the circuit at this second and third level, taking the assistant to the assistant into his confidence. As Fowler puts it, "These men are in these jobs because someday they will take over the head of the department. They may take over the department the day my project comes up for approval. It's too late then to tell them about it."

Ted Fowler, with all sincerity, believes that if his plan can stand the test of all this scrutiny belowdecks, it's a leadpipe cinch to be approved on the bridge. Fowler will also go to great lengths to see that Mr. Cox's secretary understands the idea.

It's surprising how important it is that Miss Shuler refer to it in front of Mr. Cox as "Mr. Fowler's big project" instead of as "that Fowler thing."

Fowler during this time has not been selling hard, just quietly. Almost diffidently as if he didn't know whether they'd be at all interested, but "what do you think of it?"

But an amazing phenomenon now begins. At the end of a week on all floors from the first to the twenty-first there has developed a whole debating society of people who are aware of "The Fowler Plan." Like the ubiquitous Kilroy . . . "Fowler was here."

Though it was only an idea that began in the head of Ted Fowler it has now become a "thing," a project, invested a little with the character of an accomplished fact. Since everywhere you go you meet people who know about "The Project," you never ask, "Whose idea is this?" It seems already so well established that you assume this came down from top level. You assume it's beyond the question stage. You are apt only to ask, "When does it happen?"

Fowler's name begins to disappear from it. This is Fowler's doing. When he talks about it he is apt to attribute the idea to Mr. Blaw who may have a long time ago made some remark which stirred the idea in Fowler. As he proceeds, other people add ideas to the main idea. Fowler liberally quotes these people and credits them. The man so credited is proud of his part of it. And so many people have had a part of it that they constitute a large body of support.

You can see how The Fowler Idea gradually changes

to THE IDEA and how it bolsters its way upstairs and finally lands on the agenda of the spring meeting of the Board of Directors.

Now the Board never heard of Mr. Fowler. But when the directors query management on this idea (it doesn't matter which department they ask) every top level of management knows about the plan . . . and to the Board it looks like a unified request from a demanding management.

Fowler has "touched every base."

26

How to Close a Conference

THE MOST IMPORTANT PART of a conference is the end.

Sometimes the last few minutes can dissipate all the good that was accomplished in the meeting. Sometimes the final few minutes can salvage a failure.

Chiefly to be avoided is a fizzle-out ending:

"Well, we've explored the subject thoroughly."

"Well, we'll talk it over again."

"Well, we'll work it out all right."

These are fizzle-outs. They lead to no action. Talk is nothing, unless electrical vibrations have some academic interest to you.

If some of the members left early, the meeting fizzled out. The remaining men usually know or suspect that any decision reached without the early-leavers is shaky and subject to audit and reversal. Their departure also instantly tags the meeting as "less important," which is an unhealthy atmosphere in which to sell a product or an idea.

The time to prevent such an early exodus is *before* the meeting. It goes back to the prior planning we talked about before. If you suspect one of your men is planning to leave early, call him or meet him in the hall. "Ed, I know you have a tight schedule. But I'd like to have you stay through the meeting tomorrow. Need your help."

If the meeting devolves into a cluster of private conversations which finally infiltrate out into the hall in twos and threes—failure.

When the desire to avoid repeating certain harsh assignments, realities, prices or conclusions causes the spokesman to trust to luck that all have understood their separate parts of the bargain, the meeting has probably failed at the ending.

The very reluctance to repeat the specific conclusions reveals to all that the followup will be lax and timid, that the meeting was not binding.

Ray Culley, president of Cinécraft Productions, Inc., closes any meeting with a crystalline summary. He does it almost by reflex. His method may be too studied for your particular use. But it is no doubt adaptable to your own character.

Culley verbally counts them off on his fingers. "We've decided then that Cinécraft will deliver a finished film by November 8th. Price $72,000. Geoffrey & Lamson, the agency, will furnish one man to accompany our crews as technical adviser starting August 5th in Montreal. The Steel Company will clear our crews to enter all their plants by the same date. Very good, gentlemen. Let's go to work."

And when he's through, every man knows explicitly what he's bargained for; and they usually like it that way.

When a meeting has ended it's usually a good idea to leave it ended. Often, after a tough verbal struggle, when the point has been won or lost or compromised, the parties involved are inclined to go drink a toast to each other in the nearest tavern. At this precarious juncture, as the people are leaving the room, some very smart or very obtuse gentleman is apt to remark, "Say, we didn't take up the matter of who's going to furnish the transportation on this job."

But to go back into that room now is like washing the dishes after the company has left. If it's possible to dispatch the matter without reconvening you may be much better off. And you can usually handle it by assuming the problem yourself: "Suppose I work out a plan on that and check with each of you by phone. Will that be all right?"

You'll usually find no objections. *Put yourself in the other men's shoes, and the argument is over.* In fact that is a one-sentence summary of this book.

27

A Word in Private

We would have one last word with the man who wants to get ahead in the business world or any other.

It's a private word, because the things we have to say are not talked about in public.

A strange virus has infected the American scene in recent years. You might call it negativism. You could hardly call it cynicism because it isn't that honest. It is rather a kind of sophomoric sophistication that makes it unfashionable, any more, to speak as though you have faith in anything. In the best circles men no longer talk about their great dream of accomplishing something great and good in this world. To do so is to lay yourself open to sarcasm and ridicule.

Because of this widespread attitude people are going around with their dreams locked up inside themselves, making a career of showing how much they don't believe in.

This is bewildering to everyone who has such dreams.

He wonders if there isn't something wrong with him, because he thinks the way he does. It's hard to keep the dream alive in this desert of cultivated cynicism. It causes us to look at the successful person with some distrust because we are never quite sure his success did not come from clever manipulation in this social shellgame. We don't want to believe this is how people get ahead, but dammit, it could be.

Well, we have something to say to you on this subject; and all that has gone before in this book was by way of leading up to it. You will have noticed a certain flipness of style in some of the preceding chapters which may have seemed to you typical of the cultivated cynicism we are talking about now. This was a rather deliberate effort on our part to speak in the current vernacular, to get past first base, you might say, with certain of our overindoctrinated readers.

But the fact is that 99 and 94/100th of the people you'll meet in conference really do believe in something. They really do try to perform their everyday tasks a little better today than they did yesterday. They really do admire the man who works hard to achieve a goal that is worth the title.

There isn't much talk about this. None of us likes to get caught with his heart showing. We all believe in the old-fashioned virtues of honesty and diligence and hard work and plain speaking; we're just afraid to show it. We needn't be. Because the others around the table feel the same way. A little naked idealism lying out on the conference table, backed up by a good strong jaw, will carry the day 'most every time.

You can put your faith in the decency and honesty of the people you work with. You can argue enthusiastically for the things you believe in and you can expect everyone around you to join in the common effort to accomplish things which are good for the operation and everyone connected with it.

Are we saying now that there are no opportunists in the world, that there are no selfish people around that conference table who will rise at the expense of someone else? No. In truth such people do exist and in great numbers. We say only that they can do no permanent harm to anyone except themselves. We say they can be safely ignored, and must be ignored. Otherwise our energies are spent in resentment, jealousy or retaliation. These can be poison to the conference and to a career.

Do your job with all the eagerness and enthusiasm you can put into it. The shellgame artist two offices down is a concern of yours only if you allow resentment of him to deflect you from your course.

If you need fortification for your hopes, study the careers of the really successful people around you. You'll almost inevitably find that they were plain-dealing men who didn't outsmart everybody else, but just outworked them.

Sometimes, when logic is against you, try emotion. You'll be amazed at the power of your own enthusiasm and your willingness to express it.

And how does all this apply in the conference? Well, simply this way. Bring your enthusiasm to the conference table. Show a little of your heart once in a while. Don't be afraid to speak up for something you really believe in; and let everyone know how earnestly you believe it. This can be contagious. It can carry the whole group.

And if the negative conversation you hear on your way to the meetings becomes too overwhelming, fall back on a favorite quotation of ours:

> All that is necessary for the triumph of evil
> is that good men do nothing.
> > —Edmund Burke.

Good luck,

> *William D. Ellis*
> *Frank Siedel*